HERE

×

"Elsewhere: Here"
Various
First Published 2012

Published by Cargo Publishing & McSweeney's
978-1-908885-05-0

Bic Code-FA Modern & Contemporary Fiction
FYB Short Stories

Published in association with the Edinburgh International Book Festival, with the support of Creative Scotland and the Scottish Government's Edinburgh Festivals Expo Fund.

Also available as:
Ebook
Kindle ebook

Printed & bound in China by Shanghai Offset Printing Products Ltd.
Cover illustrations by Jack Teagle
Designed by McSweeney's

www.cargopublishing.com
www.mcsweeneys.net
www.edbookfest.co.uk
www.jackteagle.co.uk

BE HERE NOW

by MIGUEL SYJUCO

IT'S EXCITING TO get to know your new kitchen and its appliances. The white promise of the stove-top.

A microwave with unblistered buttons and walls still spatterless.

The fridge unburdened, free of the steeped scents and mysterious residue of condiments collected in the ridges of the shelves. Swing open its door and it's as if the bulb was always on, like a welcoming porch light; the half-emptied boxes of kung pao chicken, spring rolls, and chow mein echo those larger ones labelled, stacked, and half unpacked in the bedroom, the hallway, the open-concept living room.

Jenna hangs a painting on a wall. Jenna asks me if it's straight. Jenna has a hard time figuring out the latch before opening the window. In rushes night air and the plaintiveness of a guitar being played by a distant neighbour. Something sets off the motion-detector light in the backyard next door and Jenna is beautiful in its illumination. Still hungry? she asks me. Just looking at my new fridge, I tell her. I close the door and the kitchen is dark and unfamiliar again. Ow, fuck, I stubbed my toe, I say to Jenna, and she puts down the tinkling box of light bulbs and comes to me to wrap her arms around my neck and quietly whisper thank you for doing this.

We spent yesterday afternoon writing my father's name on labels and sewing them onto his clothes. We rushed to check out from our motel and deliver his suitcase before visiting hours ended at the residence. He just stared out of the window in his room, pretending he'd forgotten who we are, refusing to acknowledge us when we spoke to him. Jenna and I drove the five hours home squinting into the descending sun. She rattled off rationalisations for me, as if singing to music. I looked at her often, to try to remember always how the sun lit up her green eyes. On the way, we got lost. We argued, my map-reading skills stubborn against her knack for recognising landmarks. Even when we accidentally found our street, we couldn't distinguish our bungalow from the others. We'd forgotten what number it was. In the end, we knew our home only because it was the only one that was completely dark.

Jenna asks me if I want to smoke a joint and explore the neighbourhood. I tell her I'm too exhausted for anything but hitting the sack. The only thing more tiring than a Saturday spent packing is a Saturday spent unpacking. Her job at the conservatory starts Monday week. In the alcove off the living room, her bag of books and supplies sits beside her desk, like a schoolboy sulking over the last days of summer. I stand over the desk and fire up my laptop. Hey, I call out, unprotected wi-fi from next door! Jenna peeks out from the bathroom and pulls her toothbrush from her mouth to smile widely. She clears her pile of clothes from the office chair and wheels it over. There, she says proudly, make yourself at home. She tousles my hair. She tells me she put in the mattress topper and bed sheets. No more sleeping bags, she says. Memory foam, she says, trying to entice me. Costco's best, she says. I'm not yet tired, I reply, I'll be along soon, it's not even eleven. She looks at me as if I'm hiding something but decides against saying anything. She kisses me on the head and retrieves her stack of bridal magazines from her desk. She closes the bedroom door behind her.

It's good to be home, even if home is unfamiliar. Jenna had done all the packing while I was away shooting. All last month, each time we Skyped – her bedtime, my dawn – I saw our apartment progressively stripped of its familiar Ikea items, cardboard boxes slowly accumulating behind my fiancée. Then there was her frantic call while I was covering a pro-democracy rally – the movers hadn't shown up, the new tenants were moving in the following morning. Then the sad text messages all weekend – she was driving from our city of five years, en route to somewhere entirely new to us both. Those brief moments of connectivity with Jenna grounded me, and for the first time in my life I felt the pull between where I was and wasn't. Somewhere beyond my thrill of being so alive in a place of everyday death, beyond the adrenaline, beyond the confidence of a noble cause, the home Jenna and I had built was being dismantled for lives moving forward and I wasn't there to be part of it. Never had I understood the soldiers and aid workers better, even if we were opposites, they impatient to change things while I rushed to capture things before they could be changed. The photos Jenna had emailed of the houses we could choose as ours, their bathrooms brightened by flash and a tantalising fragment of Jenna chanced in the mirror, served to both highlight the bloodshed and make it more unreal and therefore more bearable in the images I was preparing on my laptop to send to the wire service. Even though I had been on those streets only hours before, the quotidian horrors – the toddler with feet blown off, the stacked bodies almost made anonymous by ubiquity but for the anguished embrace of relatives – all felt as if from some Hollywood flick recently seen at the theatre. We all have ways of coping, of sublimating or acting out, but Jenna's constant activity in the margins of my days and nights simultaneously soothed me and made me fear for our lives.

I check my email. I'm relieved and disappointed there's nothing. I browse through some of my photos that made front pages.

A soldier on his knees defusing an IED on the roadside outside a school, the swings in the background moving in the wind.

A row of local soldiers facing off with angry residents who point and curse at them.

A group of boys hiding behind mothers and sisters dressed in niqabs, the women's eyes expressive against the expanse of black cloth.

I showed those pictures to Jenna over dinner tonight. She said she was proud of me. I'm proud, too, though I often fight the feeling I've grown into a vulture. Colleagues tell me I shouldn't think too much, but that strikes me as wrong. It's our responsibility to think, and it's our victory to bear it. I do take comfort in the old idea that we must witness suffering so that it may not be repeated. But callousness and naivety make strange bedfellows.

I know I won't be able to sleep. I know by experience that it takes at least a week to negotiate the limbo between this world and the one I've left behind. Usually, as now, I say it's jet lag. Every day we fool ourselves, though some of us are more deserving of illusions.

I surf the net. I check my email. I'm like a smoker jonesing for a cig, the online connections like a rush of nicotine after a flight or a meeting. The headlines on the news sites are the same variations – a bombing in the Middle East, a school shooting in the Midwest, an earthquake in Northern China – recurrences now too foreign and too familiar to me. To us.

Twitter is a burst of noise that I can't negotiate right now.

The Craigslist classifieds offer free stuff. Crap I don't need, crap I want but don't have space for.

Bamboo blinds.

Broken dishwasher.

Plaid couch.

Tail lights for a Jetta.

Air hockey table with only one paddle.

It's a shame Jenna won't appreciate a stuffed moose head in our living room.

Wood pallets.

A boulder? There's even a picture of it. It's round.

I have a photograph somewhere of myself as a boy standing

with my grandfather on a similar rock, taken in a valley in the Rockies of eastern British Columbia. I was too young to form an indelible memory of that time, though the picture and my parents' stories have convinced me I remember it well. I can't recall touching my grandfather in his coffin a couple of years after that picture was taken, though my parents tell me I did; but I have somehow retained, or maybe formed, a memory of standing on that rock, holding my grandpa's hand. I know what his hand felt like at that moment, its skin dry and rough like a corkboard, its flesh soft beneath as if already falling away from his bones. I remember visiting the site of the internment camp where he and my father had lived for four years. I'm not sure if my memories are of that very day or of my parents' recounting of it, but I know I walked in what was by then an anonymous field along an unremarkable road. I can close my eyes and see the boarded up building where my grandmother stood outside and told me it was there where the guards would look at her with with anger and disappointment that she, a white woman, had come to visit the enemy. I google the name of the village and find its official website, hoping for pictures to fill those gaps in my memory. I click on a link: 'History'.

The 1890s, gold rush.

1901, Slocan becomes a city.

1921, Slocan Lake freezes over.

1947, Mrs ED Popoff elected first woman mayor in BC.

1958, Slocan becomes a village.

1989, New #6 highway completed.

2000, Springer Creek RV park opens.

No mention, no pictures, of the camp where my grandfather spent his prime, my father his adolescence.

On Facebook, I have four new friend requests. I don't know any of them. Monica Garcia has posted a picture on my wall. Who is Monica Garcia? Scrolling down her profile, I really don't remember her. Her profile pic is of her smiling, leaning into some guy who has his arms around her. There's an ostentatious pride in such photos of sweet pairs, showing off how much they believe in love. What I see is implied incompleteness, tacit neediness. I accept Monica's request, so that I can slideshow through her photos:

Monica in front of the fake Eiffel Tower in Vegas.

Monica bicycling.

Monica with a four friends at a party, each dressed as a Spice Girl.

Monica with family around a Christmas tree, everyone trying to outdo the others with hideous yuletide sweaters.

Monica carrying her infant nephew, gazing at him as if he was cute.

What is she trying to say by sharing such pictures publicly?

Look, everyone, I'm happy!

Look, folks, life has treated me well!

Could that really be true if you need to declare it? Is it less true if you need to memorialise it before it's gone? They're perfect pictures from an imperfect life. Isn't that the truth? Every time we pose for a camera we're making a wish without knowing it.

I click on what she's posted. It's an old photo of me. I look so young. I always posed that way – brazen, insouciant, like someone who is asking to be punched but hasn't found any takers yet.

I even remember that party. This time of year many summers ago, home from my freshman year.

It wasn't the first night I'd kissed Charmane, but it was the first night she let me put my hand up her dress and a finger inside her.

I remember that dress, how, after we'd first made love weeks later, I'd picked it up off the floor. The tag read 'FCUK' and I thought, how fitting.

I remember how she held me on the back of my motorcycle, how she squealed when I popped a wheelie, how I killed the engine and coasted up to her house with my lights off, and how she took off her shoes and tiptoed barefoot so as not to wake her dad.

I remember her slender feet.

How wonderful it is to be able to say those words, without regret: I remember.

On the highway home, I made myself speed beyond my comfort zone, the thrill multiplying everything about that evening, to the point that I arrived at our driveway with my hands and knees trembling. I remember laughing at my frailty.

I remember calling her after sneaking into my own room, to tell her I arrived safely.

With memories like those, how could we have given up on each other?

I look at the motorcycles on Craigslist. I look at the personals, the Missed Connections. I look at listings for cars, houses, collectibles, vacation rentals. I check my email. On Facebook, I find Charmane's profile. Access is restricted to only her friends. I don't want to write her. Maybe I'm afraid of the decay that years will always divulge. I look up from trawling for whatever it is I'm searching for. It's nearly three. Fuck. The tea kettle and chamomile are still packed, so I go to PornTube and masturbate. I wipe myself off and check my email. I force myself away from the desk and stand outside on the uneven paving stones leading to our garage. The night is peaceful with its usual racket. I walk on our lawn. Overhead, an airplane passes sonorously, but I can't see it. I feel my way to the bedroom. Jenna snores quietly. Her face is lined in silver from the security floodlight in the neighbour's backyard that is on, then suddenly off.

The next day, Jenna lets me sleep until noon. We spend the day arranging furniture, emptying boxes, and filling rooms with framed paintings and prints, bric-a-brac, and boxes now useless. Before we know it, the day is over, and Jenna is lying on her stomach in bed paging through a magazine for wedding dresses. She looks up at me and pats the space on the bed beside her. Come on, she says, closing her magazine. Let's look at this one, she says, opening a magazine for wedding venues. She flips to the pages she's marked with post-its, displaying them like they were centre-fold models:

A village outside Avignon.

An historical hotel in New Hampshire.

A beach in Bali.

A loft with views of the New York City skyline.

I smile. I have work to do, I tell her, on the computer. I promise I'll come to bed shortly.

I check my email. I look at a couple of cartoon sites. One has an old man telling his grandson, 'When you get as old and gassy as me, the best investment you can make is a dog and a leather armchair.' I look for chrome accessories for a Vespa I don't own. On Facebook, I read the posts, statuses, and conversations from my network:

Stella is tired from work.

Kenza is now in a relationship with Phil.

Stephanie thinks sanity is overrated.

Ditto says the France-Algeria match was colonial comeuppance.

Valdes says: 'Heatwave in NYC = God's armpit.' To which Cach replies: 'Sounds like New Jersey.'

Gelareh posted photos of her new vintage outfit.

Someone I don't know, Caroline, posted photos of herself at a beach wedding.

Maria has put on something like 50 pounds since I last saw her in high school. But she looks happier than ever.

On Fran's wall, Elmer has posted a picture. It's of a framed photo of Fran placed in front of a coffin flanked by flowers. I click on it. There are 45 comments below: 'RIP Fran!' 'You were too sweet for this world, Frannie.' 'A shooting star, baby!' The posts are dated last year. I click on Fran's profile. Her main pic is her smiling while windsurfing. Her basic info says she's interested in men, and is looking for friendship, dating, a relationship, random play, whatever I can get, networking. Also listed are her past employment and current job, the schools she attended, her favourite books and bands, the quotes she most loves. Loved. She has 4,200 friends. Had. Has. On her wall, one of them has posted, 'Hi Fran, just saying hi wherever u r. We miss you. Hope ur dancing n having fun.'

I wonder how long her page will remain, how many months or years servers will keep our profiles, even when we're already somewhere else. I hope they outlast even memory.

I watch old music videos on YouTube. Journey, Queen, The Smiths. I compare reviews on Weber and Broil King barbecues.

On Craigslist, I look at the personals. Casual Encounters:

White bi-top seeks MFM w/ cuck couple.

BBC bull with 9-inch curve for BBW.

Attractive BF & GF visiting town ISO similar for same room sex or, should chemistry be right, soft swap.

I wonder how fine is the line between loneliness and lust?

I read the Missed Connections personals.

Says one: 'Hot concert security guard, sorry I laughed when you got reprimanded for letting me pee behind the equipment van.'

Says another: 'You – Sexy carpenter in ripped-jeans, smokin-ass Chevy Colorado, Joe Boxers. I could see your pecs squeezing out of your shirt. Me – 35-year-old housewife looking for a little something-something on the side. Call me. We can cuddle and watch "True Blood" together.'

I lie down beside Jenna and watch her sleeping. Her eyelids flicker with REM sleep. She smiles at something. She giggles. Where has she gone that makes her so happy? How can I get there?

Each following day passes like its predecessor:

Unpacking.

Hanging.

Arranging.

Eating.

Talking.

Avoiding discussing the wedding plans, pretending I'm a typical guy.

Sitting at the desk, mimicking work until Jenna goes to sleep.

Two days ago, the email arrived. My editor outlined my new assignment. I deleted it.

This morning, Jenna cooked breakfast for both of us for the first time since I got back. Happy Sunday, she declared. She stood at my bedside with breakfast on a tray. I said I was still too jet-lagged and I turned my back on her. I heard plates and glasses crash in the kitchen sink. We didn't talk all day. I slipped out to the garage and unboxed tools, hardware, cans of oil, antifreeze, solvents, paint. Through the window I could watch Jenna in our bedroom, arranging the closet into sections, for foldable shirts, hanging shirts, trousers, underwear.

The final box in the garage was mis-labelled. It shouldn't have been put here. I sit in front of it and unpack things one by one. My old pencil-case. Comics. G I Joe figures. Photo albums. Soccer trophies. I hold in my hand the daruma doll my father bought me on my first trip to his ancestral prefecture. It's as good as new, its red and gold papier-maché still vibrant. I place it on the floor and push it. It rolls back and forth on its heavy bottom, bowing repeatedly. One eye is blank white space, while the other is a yellow circle I drew in crayon long ago. I remember rain falling outside the market, my father explaining that darumas are symbols of good fortune and strong determination. People paint in one eye when they set out to do something, he said, and they paint in the other when that something is done. I look at the painted eye. I don't remember what goal I'd set out to pursue. I search the crayons in my pencil case until I find a blue one. Very slowly, I colour over the yellow.

Jenna calls my name from the back door. Where are you? she says. I finish redoing the eye. It's now green. Jenna calls my name. I step out from the garage. There you are, she says. She smiles. Where've you been, she says, I've been wondering why you weren't with me.

ON THE SHOULDERS OF OTHERS

by THERESA BRESLIN

WHEN THE TOUR buses halted at the cotton fields beyond Samarkand it was Ramil who was always first to break off working.

Like exotic migrant birds, tourists from Britain, America, Germany, Japan and elsewhere would swoop, flocking and chaffering, along the roadside. Often Ramil took the chance to light a cigarette and observe from a distance. No one was interested in him anyway. It was the women they wanted to see: those who still wore the traditional vibrant Uzbek dress, the dark-eyed young girls, and the older folk with their array of gold-filled front teeth.

Most of the tourists would have read up on the history and culture of Uzbekistan and absorbed the information provided by the more diligent tour guides. These foreign visitors didn't consider themselves tourists – in their view tourists went off to holiday resorts for a fortnight in the sun. They were 'travellers' he'd heard them say, and they especially wanted to visit the land of the Great Silk Road to follow in the footsteps of famous explorers, such as Marco Polo, who'd made this journey before them.

Ramil, wearing his designer logo T-shirt and jeans, wasn't worth a photograph to show back home. As usual, this group ignored him. He didn't care. It gave him the opportunity to approach the tractor drivers. Ramil finished his cigarette, picked up his almost empty cotton-collecting sack and, walking past the old man who swept up the leavings of the workers, he went to the end of the row where one of drivers stood beside the weighing machine. The western cigarettes Ramil's affluent father bought for him were visible inside the sack as he handed it over. Moments later he returned to the field with his sack empty of cigarettes but bulging with cotton – a respectable amount, so that he wouldn't lose face when it came to weighing-in time.

In this country it was all about losing face, or rather, *not* losing face. But it was ridiculous that he should be here picking cotton like a field hand for a miserable wage. His family claimed they could trace ancestry to the mighty Timur, the warrior known as Tamerlane, who'd crushed the Golden Horde and tried to forge a nation from diverse tribes. And his parents were wealthy. They didn't need to hap up their belongings and sit at crossroads with their children, waiting for the harvest hirers to look them over before deciding whether to employ them. Yet his father insisted that now Ramil was at university his son must take part in the harvest, as lots of students did, and live for six weeks in basic shared accommodation to help pick cotton.

'Cotton is vital for our economy,' his father said. 'It provides clothes and paper and soap and cattle feed and a host of other uses. The world needs cotton. It's Uzbekistan's 'white gold' and the work of those who went before you is why you're able to attend university. Young people have always helped with the harvest. It's part of your heritage, an obligation. You must go.'

With a roar of its engine and trailing a plume of exhaust fumes the bus left and the workers drifted back. Ramil inclined his head to the attractive girl he'd noticed earlier. A university student like himself, yet she was completely at ease in this environment. He gave her a small salute and she smiled and waved. Ah... his mood lifted. Although, he thought her as naïve as the rest, who never accepted money for photographs, and were just happy to see their faces on the digital cameras or to take a break to practise their English. He watched her join the women chatting about the tourists and the countries they came from.

By evening Ramil was exhausted. His city living hadn't prepared him for the sheer hard work. The prickly spines of the bolls that held the cotton fibre tore at his fingers and sweat stains were spoiling his expensive T-shirt. His fellow workers didn't seem to mind so much. Together on the seating mattresses beside the low tables spread with coloured cloth and laden with plates of pilaff and baskets full of round golden bread they began to tell stories.

He managed to manoeuvre himself next to the girl while the tales of Hodja Nasreddin, part sage, part trickster, were exchanged. It didn't matter that everyone knew these riddles and jokes from childhood. Their re-telling was like a family gathering where a familiar anecdote is anticipated with glee and laughter. Someone who'd lived in the Americas commented that similar stories existed there. After each telling people would unravel the story and discuss possible meanings and new interpretations.

Darkness came and the lamps were lit. A woman looked up at the stars blazing in the cold bright sky and spoke of the past, and of the famous scientist Ulugbek, grandson of the fierce conqueror Emperor Timur. Ulugbek didn't wish to be a warrior and became instead an astronomer. He built an observatory and accurately calculated the days of the year. He had knowledge of the planets at a time when Europe believed that a sailing ship might fall off the western end of the Atlantic Ocean.

Ramil had a sudden memory of his father taking him outside on a night much like this and naming the constellations. He'd been quite young and complained that he could not properly see, so his father had hoisted him up onto his shoulders.

Tea was poured into little bowls and distributed around the tables and then an old man spoke up, saying: 'I know a tale, but it would chill the bones of those who hear it.'

They begged him to continue. The old man drank some tea before he began:

'My story is of two men, a father and son, who ran a large roadside inn, a caravanserai, in the Kyzyl Kum desert. Their caravanserai was an important stopping place as there was no other water source available for enormous distances on every side. Caravans of rich merchants laden with silks and spices, carpets, jewels, perfume and furs passed that way. They stopped at this caravanserai where the father and his son fed and watered the travellers, camels and horses, and provided overnight accommodation for all.

'It was not unusual for traders to go missing along the Great Silk Road, and in that area they frequently did. But since time began humans have always vanished in the desert. They are prey for brigands and robbers, and also, who knows what spirits lie out there to trap the unwary? Djinns move through the desert, raising sandstorms in seconds and covering tracks. Thus travellers lose their way.'

Several of the listeners vouched that this was true. Had they not witnessed with their own eyes trailing streams of light and felt a wind arising on a calm day to stir the sand?

'Sometimes whole caravans disappeared, swallowed up by the desert. And all that could be done was to hope that they died in grace,' the old man cupped his hands to his face, 'and commend their souls to God.'

In agreement, those at the table followed suit.

'One day,' the old man went on, 'there was a fault with the water supply. The well, which was a short distance from the main building of the caravanserai, began to give off a bad smell. The water in the adjoining bathhouse ran murky and foul.

'The locals sent word to the government and, as any disruption to such important trade would have affected their income, the government immediately dispatched officials and soldiers to investigate. Beside the well the soldiers dug down to try to locate the water table and the source of the spring. Far beneath the desert sands they broke through a layer of rock and into a vast underground cavern.

'Inside the cavern they found,' the old man paused to take a sip of his tea and wipe his mouth with his scarf. 'Inside this underground cave,' he continued, 'was a... bear. A huge, blind, bear, and...' the old man looked around at his audience, 'strewn everywhere were hundreds of bones. Human bones. The remains of many, many people. Men, women and children.'

Everyone gasped. The girl beside Ramil shivered and he, quite naturally, moved closer to comfort her.

'The soldiers killed the bear and descended into the cavern. Holding aloft flaming torches they ventured deeper and found a tunnel leading to the caravanserai. At the end of the tunnel a shaft led straight up to a trapdoor in the floor of one of the cellars of the caravanserai.

'The two men, father and son, who ran the caravanserai had been stealing from the travellers. While the travellers slept they took away their horses and camels to a secret place to sell later. Then they stripped their guests of their clothes and valuables and flung them down the shaft to the bear that they kept in the cavern below.'

There were cries of horror at this vile outrage against traditional hospitality. Someone asked, 'Were the people still alive when they were thrown into the cavern?'

The old man shrugged his shoulders. 'That I do not know. In any case the men were arrested and held to await trial.'

'It's an offence not only to the travellers, but to all of us, that anyone should do such a thing to a guest,' said someone else. 'I hope these men didn't escape.'

'Indeed not,' replied the old man. 'Here now is the end of the story:

'The local people decided they didn't trust government justice. They suspected the father and son might be let off by offering to tell where the treasure was hidden or, at best, be executed swiftly. They wanted a most dreadful punishment for this most dreadful crime so they decided to mete out their own.'

'What did they do?' the girl whispered.

'A mob broke into the place where the men were being held. They tied ropes around each man's arms and legs separately and then tied the arm and leg of each man to individual horses. The horses were placed to face in opposite directions.'

An older woman nodded. 'A punishment handed out by the Emperor Timur himself to lawbreakers.'

'Hot peppers were stuffed up the nostrils of the horses and they were whipped and lashed to make them gallop away furiously to all points of the compass. And thus the father and son were torn apart.'

The girl shuddered.

Ramil drew nearer and she leaned in against him. He raised his eyes and met those of the old man: flat, almond-shaped, with the wisdom of centuries. It was the same man he'd passed on his way to bribe the tractor driver to fill his cotton sack. Ramil's heart flickered and he could not hold his gaze.

'Such a brutal punishment, such a violent end,' said one hearer.

'But they betrayed their own people,' said another.

Who are my people? Ramil thought. In Uzbekistan live descendants of not only Uzbeks, but also Tartars, Mongols, Chinese, Russians, and more.

'Who are my people?'

There was a silence and Ramil realised he'd asked the question aloud.

The women and men around the tables looked at him and then towards the old man, the storyteller, for an answer.

'Close your eyes,' the old man instructed them.

They did as he said.

'If you listen you can hear the breath of another beside you. Your neighbour. And then you may hear their neighbour, and so on, and so on. The more you listen, the more you will hear. If you listen carefully enough you will hear the whole world breathing.

'Those whom you hear breathing,' he declared, 'those are your people.'

There were exclamations of approval and delight. Ramil was silent.

The woman who'd talked about the stars said, 'It was also a great betrayal of the son by the father.'

'How so?' came the question.

'A father should teach his son to be honest and respect his fellow man.'

Ramil thought of his own father. Holding him high above his head. He must have been only six or seven, feet planted on his father's shoulders. His father's hands supporting his legs firmly so that he could see the stars.

'Come onto my shoulders, my son,' his father had said. 'I will raise you up that you may wonder at the glory of the universe and marvel at our place in it.'

The old man spoke slowly. 'If your parents teach you well, then you should not shame them.'

'And the betrayal of one's country,' added the girl, 'that too is shameful.'

'Yes, that is a terrible thing to do,' the old man agreed. 'To betray one's country and one's people. For, if one betrays one's people, one betrays one's self.' He sighed. 'How does a person live who betrays himself?'

Early next morning Ramil slid his arm from under the shoulder of the girl. She moved in her sleep and smiled. He waited until she was quiet and then left her side. He reckoned that if he moved fast and worked hard enough he could pick enough cotton to compensate for the amount he had cheated to obtain. At the door he lifted an empty cotton sack. Then Ramil went out to the fields to help gather in the harvest.

AS THE PROVERB GOES...

by ANNE FINE

Elsewhere. For me the word had a magic ring right from the start, like the beginning of a fairy tale. Once Upon a Time... Far, Far Away... Long, Long Ago... Elsewhere...

It chimed in, too, with where I longed to be at almost every moment of every day throughout my childhood. Stuck at my desk in school, I yearned to be done with the dull repetition of French verbs and tireless strictures of teachers. I wanted to be home.

At home, constantly interrupted in my reading by demands to carry laundry upstairs, put my shoes neatly in the cupboard or take my turn with the washing-up, I longed to stroll back under that cool brick archway that signalled the divide between chaotic family life and all those quiet bursts of concentration over pens and workbooks.

Things didn't change when I went off to university. It was a two hour journey home – long enough for the family you'd left to be ignored if you were happy where you were, but not too far to keep you from snatching up a bag and leaving your hall of residence on a whim if you were homesick. I went home often. But within minutes one of my parents would be nagging me to take my coat off the back of that chair and hang it on a hook, remarking (none too kindly) on what I was wearing, or reading me something from the newspaper I was just learning to despise.

And I'd start lying. 'I can't stay more than one night. I have a seminar at two tomorrow.'

Restless, my mother called me. And maybe she was right, for I am tense by nature, gnawing my fingernails until they bleed. But if it was simple restlessness then surely I would have taken much better to a married life which led to two years here and one year there, six months in this place followed by a year in that. After the seven years so many fairy tales tell us we have to wait for what we want, I jumped ship, wanting to be back where there is frost and fog and gales, and snow that comes as a surprise rather than as a settled fact of life.

So I suspect my craving to be elsewhere was something different: the sneaking, if irrational, belief that somewhere else my real true life was waiting for me – maybe in London, where I'd go to concerts every night, have lunch with my publishers, see every film; perhaps in a windswept cottage on the coast where I'd be so alone I could write longer, better books; perhaps in Seville or Paris.

Then one day, turning on the radio to hear the news, I caught the very last words of some presenter blandly wrapping up the programme before. 'So there we have it. As the old proverb goes, "Here is everywhere and everywhere is here." Thanks to my guests…'

. What drivel, I remember thinking. The sort of empty, double-ended, sub-Maharishi tosh that you might take for wisdom only if you were stoned out of your skull. I couldn't even track down the proverb. (Sayings like Seneca the Younger's 'He who is everywhere is nowhere' kept popping up, but that's quite different.) For all I know, someone misread the script, or I misheard. But still that little trail of words had put a thumbprint on my life and I began to notice the sort of small exchanges my partner and I had been having for years.

'Have I been to Sienna?' I'd ask.

'Yes. Yes, you have. With me.'

'I don't remember.'

'There was a bat in the room.'

'Oh, yes. Well, have I been to Cagliari?'

'Yes. For a festival. Only last year.'

'I thought that was in Sardinia.'

'It was.'

If you don't know where you have been, what is the point?

Then even the future started getting blurry. People would ask if I could come to supper, or give a talk. 'I'm not quite sure. I think I'm somewhere at the end of this month.'

'Oh? Somewhere nice?'

And I could barely answer, because I hadn't bothered to remember. All that I'd noticed was a rising sense of irritation at the sight of the thick black line I'd drawn across those days on the work calendar.

Then one day, proofreading a fresh edition of my first novel for adults, I came across a line I'd written over twenty years before. My hideously scarred and sexually sadistic university teacher remarks in *The Killjoy* of his quiet life: 'The more closely each of my days mirrors the one before, the more contented I am.'

Could I be turning into one of my own murderous characters? But Ian Laidlaw had been middle-aged, so maybe the burgeoning attraction of keeping life more settled was to do with that, in the same way that, as you get older, it is easier to see the point of all things quiet and still: paintings and sculptures; silence. Yet everyone else my age seemed to be cantering around the globe with even more enthusiasm than before, and even the real oldies seemed to do nothing but rush from one end of the world to the other.

No, it was definitely me. And as the days went by I realised that the haunting snippet from the radio had eaten into my soul and changed me. Now, like the staid character in Philip Larkin's *Poetry of Departures*, who feels the elemental thrill we all do when he hears the words:

He chucked up everything

And just cleared off,

but then dismisses the idea, my choice was made. The craving to be somewhere else had all but died.

And I was grateful for it – and still am, especially valuing the second half of this peculiar notion that changed my life: the part that says 'everywhere is here'. I've found that I've stopped trying to make the most of time spent in strange cities, forever hurrying off to see that art gallery before it closes, or squeezing in a visit to those ruins before my talk. I've learned the art of treating every hotel bedroom as if it were truly mine, and getting on with things I've always preferred doing anyway – writing in bed or reading for hours in the bath.

From time to time, of course, I've stopped to wonder if all I've done is grown more dull and idle, and given up on some of the richness that's out there in life. But I don't think that can be true because the magic of the word 'elsewhere' has travelled with me through this change of habit. It still gleams like a celestial city on a hill, unspoiled and unreached.

The only reason I'm no longer restless is that I now know I can take 'elsewhere' along with me.

ONCE UPON A TIME

by DEBI GLIORI

STORIES? THE IMPORTANCE of books? Don't get me started. The harder life gets, the more the need to escape. Stories offer a way out, an alternative world-view, an elsewhere that is not here and not now. Just like a drug.

Read enough of them and you'll put up with a lifetime of hell because deep down you'll be convinced that it'll all end happily ever after. Or you'll spend your life in the company of frogs because, thanks to stories, you'll believe that hidden under that amphibian skin is the beating heart of a true prince. Or you'll buy into the myth that if you're good and truthful and kind, when you die you'll go to heaven.

Oh, please. The only truth is that nobody gets out alive. Nobody.

I wasn't always like this. Back then, Air used to complain that Mac and I would believe anything as long as it came from a book. But now Air's dead, and Mac – well, Mac is elsewhere. He's so very elsewhere, nobody can reach him.

It all began, as so much did back then, with a book. To understand, you'd have to go back in time to primary school, to primary five, when Mac arrived halfway through the winter term. He was the new boy, parachuted into a class struggling with maths, English and rolling strike action that was threatening to close the school indefinitely. Mac appeared in our midst, all freckles and sticky-out joints; red-haired, bespectacled and, at first sight, one of those children sporting a sign that read 'born victim'. The Neanderthals in our class lit up at the sight of fresh meat but, to our surprise, within a few days of his arrival, Mac had everyone eating out of his hand. Mac, we all agreed, had the gift of the gab. Mordantly funny and utterly self-deprecating, everyone wanted Mac to be their friend. However, to my astonishment, Mac singled me out for the role of sole keeper-of-secrets and brother in arms. Within days we were inseparable, spending every spare moment in each other's company, sharing our deepest, secret thoughts, hopes and fears until one of us only had to think about something before the other gave it voice.

In an age before mobiles and laptops, books were our common ground. I'd always had my nose firmly buried in some story or other, and in Mac I found myself not only mirrored but magnified tenfold. Where I read, Mac devoured. I absorbed and quoted from what I discovered between the pages, but Mac ate, breathed, lived and became the stories. For Mac, the border between reality and fiction didn't exist. Or to put it another way, from the moment he could read, he'd had his head halfway down the rabbit-hole listening for the ticking of a tardy rabbit's watch. For Mac, every stand of trees was a Wild Wood, every wardrobe offered passage into another world and, if he overturned enough boulders, one day he'd be sure to find a Psammead.

As we moved from primary to high school, Mac's belief in the world of the imagination barely changed. Externally, adolescence was wreaking its usual havoc; spots, gangly limbs and crashing silences interspersed with the honks, squeaks and vocal uncertainties of puberty. But internally, Mac remained utterly true to his essential 'Mac-ness'. He was old-young, wise beyond his years and, despite being the weediest boy in our year, he attracted a disproportionate share of adoring and adorable young women. Playing Wendy to his Peter, Air attached herself to Mac and thus became part of my life too.

Like musketeers, we drew strength from our threesome. Air was tough, sassy and streetwise. She tolerated Mac's and my love of fiction, but preferred hers in the form of newspapers.

'You're havering,' she'd mutter, faced with one of Mac's more outlandish fantasies.

'Get a grip, guys,' she'd insist when Mac and I scared ourselves witless with some horror story we'd ramped up to fever pitch by our over-taxed imaginations. But in the end, all her common sense failed to save her. Air was undone by friendship; loyalty proved to be a more lethal weak spot for fortune's arrows than any ancient Greek's dodgy heel.

I said it began with a book, but in truth it began with Mac's big sister Mhairi. As we went into second year at high school, Mhairi had been about to do her final year in medicine at Glasgow University. There was an incident with a drunken driver on Great Western Road. Mhairi, cycling back from the library with her panniers crammed full of textbooks, didn't stand a chance. Death had been instantaneous.

On such tragic happenstances, entire lives spin out of orbit. Coming back to school a week after the funeral, Mac was visibly altered. We gathered round him, Air and I, trying to heal him with kindness, but we couldn't reach him. Months went by, the year turned, but Mac still failed to show any signs of recovery.

I suspect the accidental nature of his sister's death preyed on his mind; the 'what ifs' and 'if onlys' keeping him awake and angrily grieving. He refused to talk about it. His eyes were permanently red-rimmed and, if a stick insect could be said to have lost weight, Mac looked physically diminished.

'Can't even escape into a book right now,' he confessed. 'It's too much effort and, besides, none of the characters seem to make sense any more. Their hopes and dreams are just... pointless. I find myself losing interest round page fifty...'

'Try short stories,' Air suggested. 'Most of them aren't any longer than fifty pages.'

'I loathe short stories,' Mac said. 'Not even sure we've got any at home.'

But he did. The next week he was telling us what an amazing writer H G Wells was. The week after that, there was a light in his eyes that I hadn't seen since the accident. After the first anniversary of Mhairi's death, Air and I began to think the worst was over. And thus, we picked up the weft of our friendship and carried on, Mac's sister buried, his grief apparently absorbed and our whole bright future ahead of us. Or so we thought.

Winter came in hard and fast that year, the jobless total crossed the three million mark, oil prices went through the roof, the stock market plummeted and a mood of bleak hopelessness seemed to engulf the nation. Mac, Air and I drew closer together, trying to keep the shadows at bay. We reasoned that this was an adult mess not of our making and, being teenagers, we tuned it out, turned up the volume of our music and assumed that if our parents' generation hadn't totally destroyed the planet by the time we inherited it, we'd soon sort it all out.

That night, we were holed up in Mac's bedroom, but it could just as easily have been mine, or Air's. Even now, I still find myself wondering if we might have prevented what happened. It's as if by changing one simple thing, Mac and Air's story could have had a different ending. However, in this story, Air was reading the newspaper out loud, while I riffled through Mac's collection of vinyl and Mac did headstands against the bedroom door.

'The more I read of this crap, the less I want to grow up,' Air said, crumpling the paper into a ball and hurling it into a corner of the room. Mac, toes tapping out a rhythm on the door, ignored her completely and whistled tunelessly under his breath.

'Don't you think? Mac? Mac?' Air persisted.

'I do think,' Mac said, eyes still closed. 'Actually, I think a lot. I spend a lot of time upside down as well. It improves the flow of blood to my brain and therefore sharpens my ability to think, or so Mhairi says.'

Air's head spun round and she locked eyes with me. 'Says?' she mouthed, with an imperceptible jerk of her head in Mac's direction. Her expression at this point was mildly perplexed. Later it was to become confused, aghast and ultimately, blank. But for now, she was bemused. As was I. Perhaps 'Mhairi says' was only a slip of the tense. Perhaps Mac had meant to say, 'Mhairi said' or 'Mhairi used to say'. A slip, I decided, just as Mac's eyes opened and he curled up and dropped his feet to the floor, accidentally knocking half a mug of lukewarm coffee across Air and I before turning himself right way up.

'Actually,' he continued, as we mopped up the spillage, 'I've been thinking a lot recently,' and something in his eyes made me think – WHOAH, hang on – but then he was off, verbally sprinting miles ahead, each sentence tumbling out in a chaotic jumble of pseudo-science, hippy mystical shite and a slew of freaky syntactical connections that left my head spinning. Beside me, Air's head shook rapidly from side to side in a palsy of denial.

'Wait. Wait. Aw, come on, Mac. You know that's not poss – just calm it, would you?' she begged. But Mac, now started, proved to be unstoppable.

'I know. You think I'm crazy, but you don't know, you can't know till you've tried it. It's... incredible. Mhairi knows, she'll convince you. Mock all you like but once you see it... I'm telling you, it works. IT WORKS!'

It?

'It' being, for want of a better term, a time machine. That's time machine as in a device that allows the user to wilfully flout the laws of physics and enter the realm of pure science fiction. This had to be a joke. Mac was winding us up, big-time. Actually, as a wind-up, it was too good. Mac was too convincingly mad. In truth, he was scaring the living daylights out of me and, judging by Air's expression, she wasn't far behind. Enough, already. I tried for levity, and failed.

'Mac, for God's sake. You can barely make your own bed. Toast is a task too far. How the hell d'you expect us to believe you could possibly make a time machine?'

No answer, just a glittering smile and a shrug. Across from me, Air dug her fingers into her hair and hung on for dear life as if her head was threatening to blow off.

'Aw, come on. Mac… pal… I know Mhairi's death blew you apart, but this is crazy. Mhairi is dead. She isn't… You can't…'

'She's not dead,' Mac insisted. 'At least, not in the past, she's not. Don't you see? I can go back. I can be with her before the accident. I can talk to her. Ask her stuff. She showed me how to make it work. Look, I'll prove it to you. Come with me. I'll show you.' He grabbed Air's arm, his face twisted with effort, desperately searching for the words that would make us believe him. 'You can help. I want to find out what comes next. In the future. To see if we can make things better.'

With hindsight, that was the point at which I should have found Mac's parents and begged them to get help for their rapidly unravelling son. But that would have meant telling Mac that what he was describing was impossible and that we thought he was losing it. How could we, his friends, be the ones to destroy the entire fragile, tottering edifice he'd constructed to cope with the grief of losing his sister? One of the most terrifying aspects of that night was the extent to which Mac had somehow, without our noticing it, become completely reliant on fantasy. He must've spent months building an internal Mac-logic to explain how such an impossibility could work. Many years later, I learned that psychologists have a phrase for this – cognitive dissonance. It is, in essence, doing something with one half of your mind while you force the other half to look away. It is a splitting of one's person that, depending on the depth of the schism, can become a permanent feature.

As we followed Mac downstairs, with him babbling maniacally about time tourism and the wonders of the future ahead, I felt hollowed-out by fear but still hoped that somehow, miraculously, he was telling the truth. Then we were outside, Air and I still coffee-stained and damply shivering in the chill wind. We followed Mac down the path, past abandoned flower-beds, and into the garden shed.

Before Mhairi's death, Mac's Dad had made some attempt at keeping the garden in check, but the subsequent fifteen months of neglect had taken their toll. Mac flung the door wide to reveal rakes and hoes rusting on their hooks. Seeds spilled out of rotting packets and bird shit speckled the floor. In a corner, shrouded by hessian sacks, lay Mac's invention. If further evidence was needed of Mac's slipping grasp on reality, the jumbled mess in front of us was proof positive that our friend was ill and had been for some time. I saw a car seat complete with seat belt, a vintage vacuum cleaner, a dry-cleaner's bag draped over a standard lamp and a clock radio gaffer taped to the top of a computer monitor. And all around, a fankle of jump leads, cables and extension leads, all wired, taped and spliced together with no regard for compatibility or purpose.

Air turned aside, hiding her face from view, and I avoided making eye contact with Mac but, by then, he was so intent on demonstrating the effectiveness of his machine that I doubt he noticed.

'I know, I know,' he muttered, flicking switches and, to my horror, plugging something into a wall socket. 'Doesn't look like much, but just you wait till we get this baby up and running, then you'll see...'

Oh, I saw all right. I saw something I'll never forget, no matter how hard I try. Mac slid into the car seat, solemnly belted himself in, pulled the plastic dry-cleaner's bag over his head and fired up the vacuum cleaner. What the hell he thought he was doing I have no idea but, as the plastic instantly moulded itself to his face, Air leapt forwards yelling, 'NO! NO! Idiot – you'll suffoc–'

There was a blue flash, Air gave a sort of surprised half-cough, half-grunt, and then she flew backwards and crashed to the floor. She landed on one of Mac's tangles of wiring and, what with her recent dousing in cold coffee and the time I took to realise that she was actually being electrocuted and wasn't simply kicking the floor in pain and fury, she was well and truly dead.

Let's skip ahead several chapters to where Mac sits on his bed by the window. There's not much of a view, but he stares out at the courtyard where fellow travellers walk aimlessly, round and round and back and forth, smoking as if their lives depended on it. At first, I wasn't allowed to see him for fear I'd remind him of the night I lost them both. Then things relaxed a bit, and I'd cycle up after school on Fridays and make my way to the ward to see my friend. After Mac's parents died I became his sole visitor, apart from the odd aunt or social worker who'd grown attached to him over the years. So many years, now.

Air is firmly fixed in time; forever thirteen – a child compared to Mac's and my middle-age. We're the adults now, and according to the news we're still making a mess of everything. But here, Mac has the advantage. Grey and balding, Mac can time travel at will. He calls up Mhairi and Air and, judging by Mac's roars of laughter, they all appear to have a great time together. He doesn't need a time machine to go back any more. In a rare moment of clarity after some cock-up with his medication, he told me he'd downloaded a time travel app straight onto his internal hard drive which allowed him to move freely through time and space.

Which is, all things considered, just as well. Look closely and you'll see that Mac's bed has long restraining straps sewn onto the mattress. The windows in his room don't open. Occasionally, when Mhairi and Air whoop it up a bit too much, Mac ends up face-down on the floor with the duty doctor giving him an extra shot of something to bring poor Mac slamming straight back into the present, time travel apps notwithstanding.

The truth is that Mac's story will not end with a happy ever after. Although I cannot see them, I know that Mac believes Mhairi and Air are beside his bed. They watch and wait, Mhairi's arm round the younger girl's shoulders, comforting her, telling her some lie or other that she read, all those years ago, in one of the books she used to carry home from the university library.

'Once they find the correct medication, my brother will be able to lead a normal life.'

Poor Mhairi; her books say this, so it must be true.

Air leans down and pats Mac's arm and whispers, 'And when you die, you'll go to heaven.'

She is dead, so you'd imagine she'd know better than to spout this nonsense, but billions of books agree so it must be true. They removed the bible from Mac's room after he tried to eat it, page by page, but I imagine he could still recite whole chunks if he so desired. He doesn't, thankfully. Instead, he looks out of the window, at the walking lost, at the stranded time travellers smoking in the courtyard, at the dust motes caught in sunlight, at a moth struggling to free itself from a long-abandoned web.

MARILYN'S HANDS

by GILL ARBUTHNOTT

J ULIA SOUNDED ALMOST hysterical when she called. She often
sounded hyper though; you couldn't rely on it as an indicator
of her mood. I pretended to shuffle my non-existent plans for the
day so I could meet her for lunch. Maybe she'd found me some
voice-over work, or an audition. If nothing else, it meant I'd get
a decent meal.

I didn't have enough money in my purse to buy a drink, so I
waited for Julia outside the restaurant. She was twenty minutes
late when she stepped from her car wearing a suit of yellow shot
silk that clung to her artificially tautened arse as though her body
had been vacuum packed. Some of her clients must be bringing in
good money. We air kissed and she led the way in.

As we waited to be seated, I found her staring at me intently.

'What?' I asked, assuming her scrutiny implied some sort of fault. 'Did I smudge my eyeliner?'

She laughed. 'Of course not darling. Just reacquainting myself with your lovely face.'

We spent the time before our oysters arrived discussing the parlous state of the performing arts: in other words, why I wasn't getting more parts. The subject should have made Julia frown at the very least – it certainly depressed the hell out of me – but she dismissed it airily. She gave the impression of having some terrific secret that she could barely contain, but when I asked her directly, she just said, 'Let's eat first.'

It was the best – and the biggest – meal I'd had for weeks. When the coffee came Julia pushed it to one side and folded her hands on the table in front of her as though she was about to pray.

'I want you to promise you'll hear me out before you say anything, and that you'll take some time to think it through properly, whatever your initial response is.'

It was a pretty weird speech, even for Julia, and I was immediately suspicious, thinking of porn and other sordid possibilities.

'Okay,' I said cautiously.

'It's an amazing opportunity.'

I took a sip of coffee, watched her watching my face.

'Marilyn,' she said.

The coffee spilled a little as I set the cup down.

'Marilyn?' I must have looked incredulous.

'You do know what I'm talking about?'

Of course I knew. Everyone knew. Marilyn. An icon: the coveted body, the gorgeous face, the magnetic presence. Cameras focused on her alone. Anyone who shared a stage or screen with her ran the risk of becoming no more than a sentient garnish.

Until the drugs caught up with her suddenly and unexpectedly (though everyone knew she did them) and devastated her brain; finished her, mid-film.

Since then, they'd been looking for the next person to step in, take over, play the part. Play both parts: Marilyn and the role. Meanwhile the current Marilyn lay in some clinic, pierced by tubes, wrapped in sterile air, quiescent. Waiting to pass on her identity. Waiting to pass on her face.

'You're joking.'

I didn't realise I'd spoken, but the words vibrated in the air.

Julia smiled. 'I knew you'd say that, darling. Just listen and think, that's all I ask.

'You're a blank canvas; exactly what's needed. Your own face isn't well-known to the public – after all, most of what you do is small theatre stuff.'

She puckered her mouth in distaste until it looked like a cat's backside. No pretence from dear Julia that artistic integrity was more important than money.

'But I don't even look like her.'

She fiddled with her untouched coffee. 'I ran a check on the physical specs they're after, and your bone structure is a ninety three percent match. You sound like her anyway, and voice training would emphasise the likeness.

'Think of it darling, think of the future you'd have...'

'I'm not doing it.'

Julia held up her hand. 'I'm not listening to you just now. Go home and sleep on it. This is a chance in a million. I've got clients who would kill, literally kill, to be Marilyn. Think of the money, the adulation...'

'You're thinking of the money, aren't you?'

Her face closed down, and I knew I'd gone too far.

'Of course I am,' she said crisply. 'I'm your agent; that's what I do. I find you parts, they pay you, I take my percentage. That's how it works. Occasionally.'

I tried to look contrite. 'I'm sorry Julia. I'm just... the idea is a shock, that's all.'

The smile returned. She'd bought it. At least I could still act.

'I understand. Don't say any more about it now. Go home, think things through properly and I'll call you tomorrow.' She looked at me intently. 'You'd be mad to let this chance slip through your fingers. I'll set up a preliminary meeting as soon as I get the go ahead from you.'

I nodded. 'Okay. I'll think about it.'

When I got home I levered my feet out of their elegant shoes, peeled off the smart clothes and, dressed like a slob, took off my makeup. My face in the mirror suddenly looked as though it belonged to a stranger. I gazed at it, trying to see beneath the surface to the ninety three percent congruence that Julia claimed. It wasn't easy to believe it was true.

But if it was, what then? What if I chose to extinguish myself, and wear Marilyn's face instead of my own?

There would be wealth, and fame. How did I feel about that? I'd never expected to be famous; not properly famous. Truly, all I had ever hoped for was recognition, a much lower-key concept.

I'd never considered true stardom as anything more than a fantasy.

Wealth, on the other hand, was something I craved. I'd never, since I was old enough to count it, spent a week free from worry about money; partly my own fault of course – I'd hardly chosen a career noted for its financial security. I hungered not to have to calculate before I dared to buy. I wanted to surrender to whim, drown in luxury. Here was my chance. As Scarlett O'Hara said, I'll never go hungry again.

I wouldn't make the mistakes the others had made. I wouldn't succumb to drugs or self-loathing. I could survive as the Living Goddess. I could play the part indefinitely. With stem cells and hormones and God knew whatever else they used, I could be Marilyn for decades if I wanted to.

It couldn't hurt to let Julia set up a preliminary meeting. I wouldn't be committing myself to anything. I'd listen to what they had to say, then decide.

I called Julia first thing. She didn't attempt to hide her relief.

'Well done, darling. I knew you'd see this for the fantastic opportunity it is once you'd had time to think, though I was worried yesterday that you might be a tiny bit squeamish about the whole idea.

'I'll get right on to Marilyn's people. Don't go out until I call back, okay?'

Twenty minutes later she phoned again. 'We're meeting them at three this afternoon. They're losing money every day the shoot's delayed, so they want to get things moving as fast as possible. I'll pick you up at two. Put your hair up so they can see your face properly.'

The phone went dead before I had a chance to reply.

×

At exactly two Julia's car howled to a halt outside my building and roared off again as soon as I had both legs inside. She was never on time. Never. Until now.

'Right,' she said. 'I'll do the talking, you concentrate on looking like Marilyn.'

'But I don't,' I protested.

'You do on the inside,' she countered. 'Remember the importance of bone structure. Anyway, just imagine you're her and it will radiate from you.' She made what was presumably a radiating-Marilyn gesture and, in spite of myself, I laughed.

×

Marilyn's face gazed at me from every wall, larger than life; luminous, pearly, impossibly glamorous. The whole idea seemed ridiculous beneath her multiplied smiles. How could I possibly become Her?

A secretary walked us through to a conference room, and I tried to imagine myself into Marilyn. For once, Julia stood aside and let me enter a room first.

Three women, two men, their eyes focused, as though drawn

by invisible magnets, on my face. I paused just inside the door and let them look, turned my face one way, then another.

One of the women remembered her manners and got to her feet.

'Please, sit down. I'm Charlotte Aungier,' she said. We settled ourselves. 'My colleagues and I have the task of finding the new Marilyn. We have to strike a balance between speed and care, as I'm sure you'll understand.

'The documentation that Julia has sent looks promising and the voice tapes are most encouraging.'

'It's something that people have commented on all my life,' I said in my best Marilyn voice. 'It gets me voice-over work, but it puts casting agents off sometimes: too distracting, they say.'

She nodded, never taking her eyes off my face.

This is what it would be like, all the time.

'We'd like to take some shots of you now. Measurements and so on, get exact comparisons.' I nodded. 'Roger will take you along to the studio.'

The older of the two men rose and held the door for me. He left me with a couple of techs in a studio and returned half an hour later, after they'd taken what felt like several hundred measurements and photographs.

As he escorted me back, I paused in front of a photograph in which Marilyn had apparently been caught off guard, glancing back over her right shoulder, a slight frown on her face, mesmerising.

'You must know her quite well,' I said to Roger.

'I've met her often, naturally.'

'What's she really like?'

He gestured to the walls. 'What you see here.'

'But what's she like as a person? When she isn't in front of the camera?'

He looked puzzled. 'I'm not sure what you mean. She's always Marilyn. There is nothing else.'

When we got back to the conference room, it was clear that Julia had concluded her side of the meeting to her satisfaction. She beamed at me as I came back in.

'All right darling?'

'Fine.'

Charlotte Aungier said, 'I think this has been a very positive meeting. We'll have the tests we've just run analysed and be in touch with you within twenty four hours. Let me say, off the record, that I have the highest hopes that this is going to work out.'

✕

Julia drove me home at what was, for her, a moderate speed. Perhaps she was looking after her assets now that I had suddenly gained worth.

'My God, darling, that was marvellous. I just know they're going to go for you. God, isn't life incredible.'

As for me, it was beginning to sink in properly that this was really happening. I was elated, terrified, caught up in dreams of what my future could be.

✕

I barely slept that night, and went to the gym first thing to run myself properly awake. By the time I finished, I'd reached a decision. When I got back, the answerphone light was blinking.

'It's Julia. Call me.'

I didn't even have to go through her secretary. She must have been perched by the phone, waiting.

'They want you, darling. You've got it!' She warbled on happily, but none of what she said penetrated my brain. I waited for a pause in the monologue.

'Julia, tell them I want to see her.'

'What?'

'I want to see Marilyn before I decide.'

'But darling, that's not really a…'

'I won't do it otherwise.'

Julia sighed. 'Okay. I'll call you when it's arranged.'

✕

Everyone tried to persuade me not to go but, for once in my too compliant life, opposition only increased my determination.

It was Charlotte Aungier who took me, that afternoon, to the discreet clinic in the suburbs where Marilyn waited.

It wasn't such a shock to see her; I'd seen film of people in that state before. There was a tube down her throat and her eyelids were taped shut. Her hair lay flat and dead on the pillow around her. Wires led to the pads of the heart monitor, rising and falling gently with each artificial breath, and liquid flowed from a plastic pack along a snake of tubing and into a vein in her arm. I suppose I looked at her for ten minutes before I touched her. Her skin was warm and smooth and I noticed for the first time what beautiful hands she had – her own, of course.

Charlotte stood, obviously uncomfortable, near the door.

'I can't remember,' I said. 'How long did she do it?'

'Almost five years,' she replied. Her voice sounded strained, and I guessed she didn't like any reminder that she bore some of the responsibility for the ruin we were looking at.

'And she was... what... the third?'

'The fourth.' Charlotte moved uneasily towards the window.

And I could be the fifth.

'What was her name before?'

'Hilary Tyler. Her boyfriend nominated her. She was a nobody, really. She'd won a couple of beauty pageants, had a few small parts, but she wasn't really prepared for the fame.'

She had come to stand beside me, and now gave me what was meant to be a reassuring smile. 'That's where you have a huge advantage. You're already a proper actress. You know exactly what you're getting into.'

Maybe, after all, she was right. Unexpectedly, I felt more at ease about the whole thing now I'd seen her lying there.

'We'll send Julia the full contract for you to look at with your lawyers first thing tomorrow.'

'Fine. I'm sure there won't be any problems with it.'

The relief was visible on Charlotte's face when I said that. It was clear she'd expected the visit to Marilyn to send me into a spin.

I asked my final question as we crawled back through rush-hour traffic. 'I'm curious. What will happen to her after the... reconstruction?'

She frowned. 'I've no idea. I suppose they just switch everything off. There's no point afterwards.'

'No, I suppose not.'

As I got out of the car, Charlotte leaned out of her window and said, 'You're going to be a great Marilyn. One of the best.'

I kept thinking about her hands. All through that final night, I saw them over and over again. Those beautiful hands, now owned by Marilyn. I found a channel showing one of her recent films, recorded it, and watched it repeatedly, looking for shots that showed them.

This would be my reality if I went ahead. I would cease to have any point, except to be a simulacrum of Marilyn. No one would care about my hands.

It was such a long night, with no one to share it but the ghosts of women I didn't know.

And she was... what... the third?

The fourth.

And I would be the fifth.

Julia beamed at me, a champagne glass in one hand. Although Charlotte Aungier was perfectly groomed and made up, the strain of the past weeks showed in the thin skin around her eyes.

I finished painting the last nail and looked at my hands. I wanted them to be perfect, like the rest of me.

There was a knock at the door.

'That's it,' said Charlotte. 'Ready?'

There was silence as we walked on stage in semi-darkness, then the lights came up and the shouting began.

'Marilyn!'

'Marilyn – over here!'

'This way, Marilyn!'

A thousand flashbulbs went off at once.

I held my hand, my beautiful hand, in front of Marilyn's face to shield our eyes from the glare, parted her lips in that iconic smile and gave a little wave.

I am Marilyn, your Goddess. Worship me.

'Put your hand down, darling,' Julia whispered. 'They want to see your face. No one's interested in your hands.'

ANOTHER
NOT SCOTLAND

by ALASDAIR GRAY

NOBODY IS MORE like God than a baby. Babies live in eternity, a present instant tense without past, future and thought. When hungry or in pain their whole universe starves and is wholly evil until it supplies what they need, failing which they abolish it by dying. When fed, comfortable and awake they are fascinated observers of sensations, smells, tastes, noises, lights and colours. Slowly they start noticing other bodies besides their own.

As a baby I was taken out in a pram by my mother's sister, Aunt Annie, through Riddrie Knowes near my home. The Knowes had an unpaved road between big elm and beech trees, and one day (she told me years later) a crow fell into the pram from an overhead branch, perhaps struck dead by heart failure. This unexpected corpse did not hurt me, but she said that when we passed under that tree on a later perambulation I looked up as if expecting another bird to fall from it. I was obviously starting to associate ideas of things, as Hobbes, Locke and Hume called the process. More experience of the tree must have taught me it was not a dependable source of dead birds. Before my son could walk or talk I saw him too start connecting past and future. When fed his first spoonful of ice cream he frowned – What is this? – then looked shocked – It freezes! Hurts! His face tensed, mouth opened as he drew a deep breath to bellow his rage out, but stopped before the cry emerged. His mouth was thawing the freezing cream, the pain of his cold palate giving way to a wonderful new sweetness on his tongue. He swallowed, licked his lips, opened his mouth for more. The second spoonful made the first range of expressions happen again, but faster. When all the ice cream had been eaten he was welcoming the chill as herald of something good. Remember and anticipate – in other words, to think.

Wordsworth is surely right to say natural things like rainbows, sunlight, storms, flowers, etcetera appear more wonderful in our youth. So what causes our early appetite for tales of magic gifts, impossible monsters, fantastic kingdoms? I seem to remember that no sooner was home a familiar place to me than I wanted stories about extravagantly different places. In the 18th and 19th centuries some authors decided that respectable people's children were having their minds filled with unrealistic nonsense by superstitious nursemaids. They wrote tales for children about children in a world superficially like their own, where children who lied or stole came to bad ends, and good children sometimes suffered unfairly, but were at last rewarded or died and went to

Heaven. The sensible Christian poet Sam Johnson and scatter-brained Romantic poet Sam Coleridge both hated such moral tales. They agreed that young children needed tales of giants and magical wonders, 'to stretch their little minds' said Johnson. Infants live in a world of giants where even those only a year or two older tower over them. They can hardly ever redress unfair treatment so of course like imagining help from fairy godmothers, a Wizard of Oz, a magic lamp or tinderbox. As a child in the 1930s and 40s I gloried in such stories and the Disney movies based on them, which, despite ending happily, wisely contained believable nightmares – the wicked witch's gloating mockery of the skeletal prisoner dead from thirst, Dumbo Jumbo's mother chained up as a mad elephant when she revolts against her child being made a clown, Pinocchio growing donkey ears and tail after an orgy of vandalism. My appetite for such fantasies was healthily abated between the years of eight and ten when I lived at the edge of a Yorkshire market town.

Our home was a bungalow at the side of a rural lane. On the other side was a neglected field with trees and clumps of bushes, also an overgrown garden with a draw-well smothered in ivy. I recall no sign of a house, not even a ruined one. Here with one or two school friends I made what we called dens – secret places in the middle of bushes or up trees which we wanted nobody else to know about or discover. A lot of good, open-air exercise was got by trying to make these, and exploring the banks of the river Wharfe in search of others. I remember nothing remarkable happening in these dens, not even stories we told each other there, but in 1944 my return to the Glasgow housing scheme where I had been born felt like a confinement. Dens could not be built in Riddrie Knowes or our public park. Other Glasgow boys of my age played outdoors by kicking balls about. I did not enjoy that. Stories about fantastic secret lands became my obsession. I visited Riddrie Public Library four or five times a week, never taking much more than a day to finish a book.

The genre I preferred always began with someone who seemed, like me, in a world regarded as commonplace, and then found an exit into a place of magic adventures. The earliest classics of this kind were Lewis Carroll's *Alice* books, with others I read or heard dramatised on the BBC's Children's Hour – *The Magic Bed-Knob*, *The Wind in the Willows*, *The Box of Delights*. A subdivision of this genre had children who discovered lost or hidden lands when on holiday. Enid Blyton wrote a shelf of books about children finding mysterious geographies – *The Valley of Adventure*, *Sea of Adventure*, *Castle of Adventure*, *Island of Adventure*, etcetera. Growing older I found similar books had been written for adults – Conan Doyle's *The Lost World*, Rider Haggard's *She*, *The Return of She* and *Allan Quatermain*. There were films about them – *King Kong* and *Lost Horizon*. In a BBC radio dramatisation I heard H G Wells' *The War of the Worlds* and at once ordered through Glasgow Public Libraries all his early romances, which I still think are science fiction's unsurpassable best. His *The First Men in the Moon* took me to an impossible moon, yet imagined with such inventive detail that, from it, humanity is shown in a new light. That novel, *The Time Machine* and *The War of the Worlds* describe exotic worlds elsewhere, but are no more escapist fiction than *Gulliver's Travels* and Orwell's *1984*.

Before leaving secondary school I decided to write a book about a world of my own invention that would also satirise the world I knew. When planning it I was inspired by Kafka's *The Trial*, with Edwin and Willa Muir's foreword saying that Kafka's protagonist was seeking salvation like John Bunyan's Pilgrim, but in a world where neither Heaven nor Hell are signposted. In Kafka's world the agents of an obscure but inescapable bureaucracy hound a man in his rented bedroom, in the attic of a slum tenement, in the cupboard of a bank where he works and in a cathedral outside service time – encounters that I felt could happen in Glasgow. Kafka's bureaucrats were more humane and believable than Orwell's Thought Police, and his hero, K, was so ruthlessly selfish that I never doubted his guilt. I was also reading books about the growing pains of men in other cities nearer my own in time and space – *David Copperfield*, *A Portrait of the Artist as a Young Man*, *Sons and Lovers*. I now saw that books which (Milton says) the world would not willingly let die, must contain real local experiences such as those Dickens, Joyce and D H Lawrence suffered, even if combined with Heavens, Hells and Wonderlands elsewhere. Most books in the Bible did that, most folk tales and the Scottish Border Ballads. In a public library (Denistoun, not Riddrie) I found Tillyard's *The English Epic and Its Background* which, after briefly surveying the great epic poems and histories of Greece, Rome, Italy and Portugal, concluded that since Milton's time, great epics were likely to be written in prose. He said that Walter Scott's best novels almost amounted to a Scottish national epic. So that was what I set out to write.

My Scottish primary and secondary schooling had said hardly anything about Scottish culture. Our state schools before the

1970s had generally better standards than their English equivalents, but aimed to qualify the smartest pupils for high positions in England, Canada, Australia and elsewhere, so in Scotland English literature was taught as if no Scot had contributed to it. We knew of Robert Burns because many of our parents admired his poems which were also sung on the BBC Scottish Home Service, but R L Stevenson was dismissed as a writer for the very young, and the only Scott novel given to us was *Ivanhoe*. This tells how the Normans in England became acceptable to the conquered Saxons – a fine lesson for Scottish children! For most of the 20th century Hugh MacDiarmid was ignored as a poet by British academics and dismissed as a pest by Scottish politicians, though professors of literature in Europe and the USA paid attention to his work. In 1958, *The Private Memoirs and Confessions of a Justified Sinner* by James Hogg was reprinted with a preface by Andre Gide. It came to Glasgow Public Libraries and me, proving that Scottish local and supernatural events could combine in prose as well as poetry. But to work well in a book, the Scottishness of Scottish characters must be taken for granted. Dostoyevsky slightly spoils some great novels with sentences about Russian-ness. *Gillespie* by MacDougall Hay is a nearly great novel. It describes a dull but cunning, mean, greedy grocer becoming wealthy in a Highland fishing village, blighting lives around him as he does so, yet his insensitivity is almost heroic in its scale and effects. This account of 19th century capitalism transforming a small town would be almost as good as Hardy's *The Mayor of Casterbridge* and Brown's *The House with the Green Shutters*, had it not an absurd first chapter indicating that the weird, uncanny Scottish setting had doomed Gillespie's parents to produce a monster. I saw that the local setting of my epic, like the supernatural parts, must be shown through convincing details without trying to describe a national state, often represented by a noun ending in ishness.

I was 44 in 1979 when this novel was completed and accepted by an Edinburgh publishing house. I did not foresee it would be a successful book and two years would pass before it was printed, but I knew that shelves in a warehouse and shops would soon hold well-bound, hardbacked copies of *Lanark*, each 560 pages and each almost as solid as a brick. This gave me a strange but pleasant feeling that my soul – my inner being – was now safe outside me and could outlast my body. This safe feeling was helped by a new job that, in return for a little agreeable work, gave me a steady wage and an office with a view across Kelvingrove Park. I was writer in residence at Glasgow University, discussing the writings of a few students who wanted my advice, but the job did not require me to write anything. Nor did I wish to write. I had no ideas for other stories, had no intention of seeking them. I decided to enjoy reading for its own sake as I had done as a child. No longer interested in escapist fantasies, I bought Ezra Pound's complete *Cantos*. I had gathered that they were great poetry about the good and bad monetary roots of our civilisation, something we should all understand. Democracy is impossible if only economists and a few politicians understand it, as seemed to be the case in Britain. The Glasgow of my youth had been the most industrially productive part of Scotland, making and furnishing locomotive trains, ocean liners and war ships, most of the latter ordered by the British Government. Despite local protests, Glasgow was steadily losing all its industries while the British government spent more and more of our money on nuclear submarines based in the Holy Loch, again despite local protests. With the *Cantos* I also bought *The Road to Xanadu* by Livingston Lowes, a study of how Coleridge had come to write his greatest poems. I was interested in how the minds of poets work.

Alas, I found Pound's *Cantos* impenetrable, apart from his verses saying how good craftsmanship was blighted by the extortionate money lending which Marx called Capitalism. His quotations from Chinese and Renaissance scholars and founders of the USA republic, and references to Mussolini's public work schemes, produced in my mind nothing but a formless, confusing fog. But suddenly one line from his Chinese *Cantos* spoke to me clearly:

Moping around the Emperor's court, waiting for the order-to-write.

The last three words were hyphenated because they were obvious translations of a single Chinese character. I imagined a highly hierarchic empire training a man from infancy to be a great poet, flattering him with high rank and privileges, yet not letting him write a word before it ordered a great poem from him. A comic idea! I lifted a pen and wrote this –

Dear mother, dear father, I like the new palace. It is all squares like a chessboard. The red squares are buildings, the white squares are gardens...

– and started inventing another world elsewhere. Livingston Lowes' book had stimulated this by listing the exotic domains that had inspired Coleridge: a source of the Nile, a Himalayan grotto, the happy valley where Abyssinian kings kept their heirs, the artificial paradise in the Atlas Mountains where assassins were trained. This revived in my middle-age the pleasures of childhood den-making and the lost worlds that had long ago entertained me in books, comics and films. Loading my poet with madly luxurious apartments, gardens and servants, I invented the cruel education that had qualified him for these privileges, and later revealed the huge confidence trick through which the vast, exploitive empire was ruled, since the Emperor turns out to be a puppet managed by ventriloquists. I finally thought of the order-to-write – a poem praising the government's worst atrocity, the destruction of the city in which the poet had been born. *Five Letters from an Eastern Empire* is certainly my best short story.

After publication in 1983 the head of Talks in Scottish BBC Radio decided to broadcast it, and met me to discuss this. He was a pleasant man called Golding, who told me he had been placed in Glasgow with others from London to manage Scottish broadcasts in 1977, when a national referendum nearly gave Scotland a devolved parliament. When the Scottish majority in favour of this was judged too small by Westminster, Mr Golding had decided to continue living here. He asked if there was an actor I would like to read my story. 'Bill Paterson,' I said. 'But surely Bill Paterson has a Scottish voice?' said Mr Golding. I replied that Bill Paterson had indeed a Scottish voice, but there were many Scottish accents, both working class and posh. My poet was a mandarin with working-class parents; Scotland had many such mandarins in its universities, and Bill Paterson could easily sound like one.

'But your narrator is supposed to be the Poet Laureate of a great empire!' said Golding, who obviously thought the loss of the British Empire irrelevant. He had the story recorded in London by an English actor and broadcast throughout the United Kingdom.

That broadcast won the approval of Roger Scruton, a Conservative critic who thought the story a satire on Communism. A friend who later attended an international literary conference told me he had heard a Chinese and Japanese scholar discuss which of their nations my empire most resembled. I told him that, in my opinion, it most resembled Britain as a Scot saw it, or if not exactly a Scot, as a Glaswegian saw it, or if not exactly that either, as seen by a Scottish writer in Glasgow University.

ELSEWHERE IS ALWAYS WAITING

by WILLIAM McILVANNEY

S HE WOKE FROM a dream she was glad to be out of. She had been with Ray again in the old flat on the South Side. Yet nothing bad had happened in the dream. They had been drinking wine together and talking and laughing. As she lay staring at the ceiling, it was the intimacy they had been sharing that disturbed her, as if her mind were insisting that a long-past time in her life was still a part of her present, that where she was living was a more complicated place than she had thought.

She decided that what she didn't like about dreams was that they were no respecters of the reality you thought you were inhabiting. They were so subversive. They evoked places you didn't recognise or put you back in situations you were glad to be out of and made them so real that they became, intangibly but very vividly, a part of your life. They made you feel that the life you were living was not as solid and three-dimensional as you had been imagining.

Turning her head on the pillow, she widened her eyes and stared at the bedside clock, as if taking a compass-reading to fix her position in reality. On the fact that it was half-past ten the concrete present formed around her like a protective structure. It made her feel safe.

She sat up in bed and looked around her. Yes, this was where she lived, though occasionally she might wonder why. The recent activity of early morning re-ran itself in her head, like a catechism of the meaning of her life. Dave had been late for work again, using frequent imprecations like rocket fuel to propel him out of the house. The boys had been their usual sleep-walking selves: pausing, with one shoelace tied, to stare for minutes into the mystery of things, casually assaulting each other as they passed. Zac had delivered a diatribe against the unbelievable enormity of having no Sugar Puffs, maintaining with passion that all other cereals were just crap, while Michael, a lofty two years older, declared that he wouldn't be accompanying a wimp to school. No wonder she had come back to bed to cuddle into her lonely sanity.

Still, she thought (as if chastising Ray for the impertinence of his reappearance), they weren't so bad. Zac, given an unbroken supply of Sugar Puffs in his life, was one of the gentlest boys she knew. Michael was always very solicitous if he thought she was worried about something. And Dave, she supposed, was in all ways a good example to the boys.

Having gone back to bed in her bra and pants, she rose and pulled on jeans and sweater. As she did so, she changed her thought about Dave to 'in some ways'. He always seemed to turn their bedroom into a wardrobe with furniture. Yesterday's underpants were on the lid of the linen-basket, not inside it. A pair of trousers lay on the floor where he had dropped them. There was a tie over the door-handle, discarded socks beside the bed. Why did some men have to leave signs of themselves all over the place, like dogs peeing at every corner to mark out their territory? She slipped her shoes on.

She thought about tidying up the debris he had left. No. This was the case for the prosecution. She would leave it there and ask him to clear it up himself. She had to make a stand, put a stop to the idea that she was some kind of unpaid maidservant, there to follow them around and mop up after male untidiness, for his attitude had spread to the boys too. To confirm her resolution, she looked briefly into the boys' rooms as well, briefly being as long as she could stand it. There were discarded clothes and plates with congealed half-eaten food on them. Each of their rooms looked like a litter bin with a bed in it.

Coming downstairs, she noticed some pairs of the boys' shoes abandoned haphazardly in the hall. Wondering if she should leave them there as well, she was distracted by the sight of Dave's v-neck sweater lying on the hall table. It must have been too warm to wear it. Certainly, it seemed bright outside. As she lifted the sweater, she felt its fineness and thought how fussy he was about choosing clothes. Maybe he should be as fussy about other things. He had asked her to book her own birthday dinner. Romantic, eh? This was getting too much. It had to be sorted out. Beware, my family. Many things will change. Domestic Armageddon is tonight! She was walking towards the kitchen with the sweater, thinking she might put it in the wash, when the doorbell rang. She stopped at the end of the hallway and turned towards the door.

All she could see were two dark shapes, one taller than the other, through the heavy layers of lace curtains he had persuaded her to put there after they had once been taken by the urge to make love in the hallway and she had insisted on going upstairs in case someone came to the door and saw them. The situation never repeated itself but 'hope springs eternal' he had said.

She waited, watching the door. Kathleen next door had told her that two Jehovah's Witnesses had been here yesterday, a man and a woman, when she was out. Let's be out again, she thought. Jehovah at the door she could live without. But the doorbell went again. Ah well, it's short shrift for Jehovah.

As she went towards the door she quickly tried to push the shoes to the left side of the hall with her foot. That way, she half-thought, they wouldn't be visible when she opened the door, especially if she didn't open it very widely. (And with Jehovah's Witnesses that wasn't a bad idea). The door opened and she went instantly from reverie into a vivid present.

First, it is the dark, uniformed figures of a tall policeman and a shorter policewoman standing on her doorstep, black as crows. Their suddenness is startling, sheer presences stark against the brightness of the day. Panic takes her. Then she notices that old Tom Simpson across the street is mowing his lawn and her mind takes in the image like a talisman. This is where banality lives. Bad things happen elsewhere.

'Yes?' she says.

'Mrs Howard?' the policeman says.

'Yes.'

'Mrs David Howard?'

'Well, Mrs Jane Howard. But I'm David's wife, yes. What's happened?'

The man seems momentarily to have exhausted his store of language.

'I'm WPC Marion Copeland,' the policewoman says, almost making a smile but erasing it instantly. 'This is PC Bryden. Could we come in?'

They become an awkward grouping in the hall as the policeman closes the door. 'Perhaps we should sit down,' the woman says.

'Tell me what's happened.'

'I think we should sit down.'

'For God's sake, will you tell me what's happened?'

'It's about your husband,' the man says. 'There's been an accident. A car accident.'

'We need you –' the woman says.

'But how do you know it's him? How can you know? How can you?'

'He had his driving licence on him,' the man says. 'And a letter in his pocket confirmed his address. This address.'

She senses a terrible circumstance encroaching on her home and she doesn't know how to forbid it admittance.

'We need you to come –'

'But the children are at school.'

She isn't saying it to them. She is saying it to herself. It is not a statement. It is a prayer, an invocation of the power of daily things to prevent anything as unforeseen as this from happening.

'We can arrange for them to be brought home, if you want,' the woman says.

'No! Why would we do that?'

The silence that follows becomes a darkness into which it is too frightening to look. It is as if the day has developed tinnitus, become a ringing silence beyond which all other sound is distant and obscure. It seems important not to cry. Crying will admit a finality that cannot be allowed. But someone is crying and a strange voice is speaking somewhere.

'Where is Dave?'

'He's in the hospital,' a man's voice says from very far away.

A woman's face appears, strange as a gargoyle through the prism of someone's tears.

'He's dead, Mrs Howard. They think it was more or less instantaneous. I'm sorry.'

'But he just left this morning,' another voice is saying.

'We need you to come and identify the body.'

A woman is holding you. Her arms feel like a trap. To stay here is never to escape from what she is bringing. You have to be free of her.

'Excuse me, please.'

Someone you no longer are said that. It is a familiar remark from yesterday. But this is a strange today.

'Of course, Mrs Howard. We'll wait here.'

A door has closed. They are no longer there. You are alone. You must stay here. There is the novel he is reading, open on the arm of his chair. How the sunlight hits the pages. He is enjoying it. He still has to finish it. You haven't booked the birthday dinner yet. A lawn is still being mowed. How could this be happening if a lawn is being mowed? Around you the furniture seems cluttered, a jumble sale of charms. Surely they still work.

But is this still where you thought you lived? You must make this place again where you thought you lived. Touch the sideboard, feel its familiarity. Walk up and down here. The carpet feels familiar. You can smell his body in the fabric you are holding. He is still here. He can't be gone. Things are still as they were.

But how can they be, when you are crouched against a wall? This isn't where you live. You aren't who you thought you were. This is all you are, a woman crouched rocking on her haunches. Trying to measure infinity in inches.

Strange voices are talking beyond a door. They are waiting for you. They don't know that they mustn't come in. The door mustn't open. Rocking goes still. Silence means you are not.

Don't listen. If they cannot be heard, it cannot happen. Someone is knocking at a door. They do not know that you aren't here. They are elsewhere. They can't come in.

You must stay here, silent and still, or elsewhere becomes final. Let them knock.

You must stay here.

×

Creaking on the hinges he hadn't oiled, the door opened slowly.
  'Mrs Howard? Are you there?'

BILLIE D

by VIVIAN FRENCH

A T TEN IN the morning I leave my front door behind me.
Have I got my key?
What a foolish woman you are, Billie D.
The door always shuts with the same sound.
Sometimes I think my house despises me.
The mocking dust settles on all the things I hold dear
And the windows never look shiny and clear.
My windows do not twinkle at me they only sneer.

I walk tactfully down the hard grey road
Being aware of the life that is heaving beneath the paving stones.
Stones are like bones they lie without soft flesh.
I rather hope that when it all bursts out from underground

I will not be around.
There will be life in such excess
That my dry brittle mind will be embarrassed by the blood filled
    fruitfulness.

At the baker's I buy bread.
Man does not live by bread alone
Is what my mother always said
But it can go a long way towards preventing starvation and
    emaciation.
I am particularly fond of toast and jam.
When you live on your own
There is a good deal of comfort to be found in jam.
Once a great nephew came
And we had toast and tea.
Strawberry jam for him and raspberry for me.

It is still only seventeen minutes past ten.
Perhaps if I walk slowly to the papershop and back
It will take thirteen minutes more.

Time sits sullenly in the trees.
I count as I walk.
One.
Two.
Three.
Four.

The papershop is filled with fluttering words.
Side by side
Children are jittering.
Sometimes I think they don't see me at all.
Am I really Billie D
Or just a dusty shadow on the wall?
My head is not used to all the chattering
And rattles. A woman smiles at me.
I cannot reach the smile inside my head
And so she moves away.

My name is Stanley Baldwin.
I am quite used to people laughing if you wish to laugh.
My father told me that my mother had a lovely sense of humour
    which I failed to inherit.
I was born late into the night
And my mother said, 'Call him Stanley' and then laughed and
    died.
Personally I have never seen the joke.

There was a hatstand in the office where I worked.
The only other hatstand was in the office of the manager
So you can see I was a man of some importance.
Even so there was no further need for my services.
This is something I fail to understand.
Mr George had green lino and no hatstand but his services were
    still required.
This is a fact I do not comprehend.

I shall place my hat firmly upon my head and go to read The
    Times.
The quality of editing is no longer what it was
And so I do not subscribe myself.
I read the paper in the library.
I could wish that the corners were a little less thumbed.

There are cracks in the paving stones.
I do not understand why they are not filled.
Walking every day as I do one has time to observe these things.
I do not keep a car.
On occasion Mr George has offered me a lift
But I have, in every instance, declined.
Walking, I told him, one has time to observe.

I am a young person of style
I sit behind the library desk and smile
You may admire my smile when the clock strikes half past ten.
We open then.
Wet or dry the first in is the old lady
And what I say is people like that should be put away.
She's one of the ones that comes in every day
Like the other batty one, the old man.

How beautiful are my long red nails and my fingers white
Elegantly I check the books from morning to night
And watch from under my long mascaraed lashes to see what is
    going on.

I'm very quick to notice if a book has gone.

There must be something in the weather.
When I tossed back my black shining hair I saw the two old
*   things sitting together*
Or at least there was no empty chair in between.
There is no copy of The Times to be seen
Although I am sure I put it out.

Well I never. I do declare without a doubt
The grubby old thing has invited him to tea
And if my delicate ear-studded hearing did not deceive me
I heard the old man agree.

Oh Billie D whatever have you done?
There is a man coming to tea at a quarter to four
And there is dust and you have never spoken to him before.

'Would you like a cup of tea with me?'
How could I have said the words
Inside my head were the frantic featherings of caged birds
Did he agree?
Oh yes he did he did he did oh should I buy more bread?
Oh we will have toast and jam and a buttered bun
And we will talk while we drink our tea.
There is a great deal that can be said.

This is a day not like other days

Although I still do not understand why there was not a copy of
   The Times.
I have been asked out to tea at a quarter to four.
If Mr George should offer me a lift
It might be that I will take a little ride.
It will be pleasant to see what there is to see.
It would make a pleasant line of conversation
When we are talking over tea.

Oh Billie D
I have heard the church clock strike half past three
Oh whatever shall I do!
I have been glancing out of the window since half past two
And I have already sliced the bread.
He will be here at a quarter to four
And there is nothing but a hollow in my head.
I have already sliced the bread.

I put my hat firmly upon my head
At precisely half past three.
It will not take me long to reach the road in question.

There is a man walking down the road and he is coming here to
   my door
There has never been anyone here before
Except my great nephew. The one who came to tea.
I have put the kettle on.
He is knocking at the door.

There is jam in a little glass jar.
I have dropped a cup.
There are little pieces of pink china all over the floor
My hands will not pick them up.

He is knocking once more.
When will he go away?

Now I come to look
There is only jam enough for one.

I will walk slowly home
And on the way I will observe the appalling state of the roads.
I shall refuse any offer of a lift.
I will return home
And hang my hat upon the hatstand at the entrance of my room.

How the young lady with style would smile
If she could see Billie D where she sits
Picking a copy of The Times into very little bits.

A TALE OF
TWO CITIES

by YIYUN LI

I N A CERTAIN city in Florida, in the bars, there are young women sitting on high stools, and if an older man is interested in one of them, he asks the bartender to send over a cigar, and, accepting the cigar, the chosen woman also accepts drinks and a few hours of companionship.

Bolun could not remember who had told him this. He himself had not set foot in that country. In the restaurant or the karaoke bar or the spa or wherever he had heard the story, the men and women in Florida sounded as though they lived in an old-fashioned fairy tale, innocent in their roguishness and mischief.

Once in a while Bolun imagined himself the man in that fairy tale, taking his time caressing every young woman's face with his eyes. At the end of the night he might, or might not, make a move – the young women had their whole lives ahead of them. To match their patience and confidence, he too needed to be an unhurried person.

But that calmness he could only have in his imagination. The young women in the places he frequented with his business connections – misses they were called – were uniformly well-trained, and they left little space for his fairy tale. They always seemed to know what he needed; sometimes they had much more to offer than he was willing to accept.

His own wife, whom he had married twenty-seven years ago but had known all his life – their cribs had been next to each other when they had started the Little Sunflower Nursery – he no longer loved. She was not in a position to protest about that, as he had set up her boutique shop specialising in high-end stationery imported from Japan, and he had shown magnanimity when he had discovered her affair with her chauffeur. Sometimes she said that it was not healthy for a man at his age to be out drinking every night, masking, with wifely concerns, her unhappiness with the marriage. He had no other choice, he replied, sparing her his belief that he maintained his lifestyle so that their daughter, for whom he had secured a job of writing restaurant reviews for a leading fashion magazine in Beijing, would not have to make a living like the young women he patronised.

'Only a man who understands love can come up with this genius idea.' Such were the compliments paid to Bolun by his subordinates when, to advertise a new development he and his partner had built on the southern end of the sprawling metropolis, he proposed a carousel riding contest. One lucky couple – they had to be young and struggling to find a place to live in Beijing – who could beat all rivals to ride for the longest time on a carousel would take home, or rather would make a home of, a two-bedroom apartment.

Anything he proposed would be called a genius idea, Bolun knew, but this time he did love his own proposal. Very soon the contest and its logo, 'Love and Persistence Win' were printed in major newspapers. He imagined the clichés, which he especially loved: the maudlin love songs from the loudspeakers, the colorful lights lit up at night, the ups and downs of the young contestants, each couple sharing a wooden horse or a camel and burying whatever differences or disagreements they had in their relationship for the dream of having an unaffordable apartment. Bolun himself had worked all sorts of low jobs at their age. Not in every dynasty, or every country, could a man have made it as he had done, but of this he knew not to brag, as he had done nothing special. He was born at the right time and in the right place, and had recognised and acted upon a certain vague call to wealth when it was barely noticeable to most people. Take that, sometimes when he was drunk he thought of the men in the Floridian bar; now whose fairy tale was better written?

The contest began on the seventh day of the seventh month of the lunar calendar – a day associated with a love story from folklore, which had been recently revived for commercial reasons and was called the Chinese Valentine's Day. Before the first spin of the carousels there had been much publicity generated: the amusement park which hosted the contest had installed new carousels in addition to the five they had already; hundreds of young couples camped overnight in line to register for the contest; the eruptions of arguments and shedding of tears by those whom the amusement park could not accommodate were reported in the newspapers. All went as planned.

Among the excitement and chaos, one girl's story caught Bolun's attention. A recent graduate from university and a new arrival in the city, she broke up with her boyfriend of three years when he had refused to make himself 'a clown to amuse some rich men's nonsense', as the newspaper quoted him. She advertised on her blog for a new boyfriend with the stamina and determination to win an apartment with her, and even that became a contest of itself: her well-publicised first dates with her candidates fanned the PR fire for the contest.

Bolun wanted the young woman to win. She was not the prettiest, and the boy she had chosen was not the most handsome, but Bolun loved her face, where youthful dreams had died before their time and signs of suffering from a life she was too young to understand had not yet set in. He could have given her, through the PR company, a small amount of money for more presentable clothes in front of the TV crews and photographers, but that, on his part, would be a pre-emptive move of impatience.

The contest, in the end, was one of those fairy tales that went slightly wrong. For days, the carousels spun from morning till midnight, with three ten-minute breaks built in for the contestants to rest; every day more couples dropped out with paled faces but there were the persistent ones, who had to be peeled off the wooden animals with a guarantee they could resume the next day. On the seventh day, it was apparent that the eight couples left would only drop out when death interfered. The company quoted health and humanitarian concerns to end the contest without deciding a winner. It had gathered enough coverage, in any case, and each of the eight couples would get a check for twenty thousand yuan as their prize – a decent move on the company's part, as the combined total was the price of an apartment on their list.

Bolun often thought about the girl who had not won the apartment – sometimes as a father, though a father would be more heartbroken than he himself felt; sometimes as an older man would have thought of the young women on their high stools. Had they been living in one of those old-fashioned fairy tales, he would have seen to it that a cigar, a drink, a small offering be passed to her, but they were not in Florida, where palm trees clamoured with their long, finger-like leaves; they were in a city called Beijing where, as a young man, he had planted young trees that later, as a real estate developer, he had ordered to be removed.

APPARENTLY

by KAREN CAMPBELL

Y OU ARE STANDING in a garden, crying.

This morning you watched your grandmother push scraps from the breakfast plates into a Tupperware bowl. *Lena can have this for lunch.* Tough rinds of bacon tumble onto a piece of yolk your father has dipped his toast in. The dirty knife from one of the plates keeps scraping until the plates are virtually clean. Food fit for a cat. Lena is their servant. She's one of the women your grandmother's been teaching English to, in secret, arranged through the Anglican church. There was news about it on the BBC, before you even got here – rioting in Alexandra because they were being made to learn in Afrikaans. Whenever South Africa is mentioned, you tend to tune in. You have family there. And you told everyone at school about it; how gran's house was turned

by secret police, they huckled her and her friends into a van
and interviewed them downtown. Your grandmother is a white
woman. She was given a room with a chair.

Rebel gran, who's scraping plates and listening to her neighbours tell jokes about kaffirs as Lena polishes around them, her
shy, downcast skin bright with sweat. It's not how you imagined,
here. Oh, the sun is huge and raw with heat, dry granular grass
and mealies on the braai make you know you're not at home
and everything is out of date. Melamine shop frontages decked
in chirpy sixties lettering, the men all congregating in one room,
smoking while the women wear make-up and high heels. Plastic,
chunky ones which match their oversized jewellery. The white
women that is. The only black lady you've seen up close is Lena,
and she's in blue nylon, a pallid dustcoat which makes her gleam.

Not your rebel gran either. She wears soft-draped colours of
heather and moss, and flat, flat pumps which accentuate her tiny
frame; the delicate stalk for her bubble-permed head with its fine
jaw and the African hoops at her ears. There's a distinct tinge
of purple in those curls too. You love purple, it's your favourite
colour. You watch her clip the lid on the bowl and tell Lena to
take it. You hear her call her *girl*.

Now clean the floor, girl. This whole house needs redding.

Her voice goes loose and guttural, cracking back to the accent
of her past. Today is the last day of 1983; the house zings with
activity and rush. At home, it would be Hogmanay, and you hear
your mother trying to get the neighbour to pronounce it right.
Not hodge. No, hog. As in pig. You bite your smile because she
really does look like a pig, this woman. She's large and blonde

and pinkly orange, hails from Huddersfield but came here twenty years ago *on a ten pound ticket and she's never looked back, has she Jean?*

Vaguely, your gran trails a *no*, goes on chopping turnip. Or it could be pumpkin; it's the same colour as the neighbour. More stringy.

Standard of living's so much better, in't it though? I mean, we couldn't afford an house like this back home. Nor servants, eh? Although you can never trust the kaffirs, love.

She pats your mum's hand as she speaks.

So long as you know these girls'll thieve from you given half a chance, you'll do alright. In't that right Jean?

What's that? says your gran. Even now you can see her, considering the blue of the sky outside. She's an artist. Her lush paintings decorate all the walls. You decide, when you go to the game park next week, that you'll take your pastels with you. You'll draw one of those thatched huts gran showed you in her *Kruger Safari* brochure, and you'll sketch Lena sitting outside. This is your first Christmas in a foreign country and, so far, it's been very weird. Turkey dinner by the swimming pool, meeting cousins and aunts you've never seen. Observing the warp in your dad's face as your uncle and gran talk about a trip she took to Durban last year. Your uncle lives in Durban, has told you all about the shark nets, how safe it will be when you swim there. The nets are interlinked on the white beaches, sporadic on the Asian ones, non-existent for the blacks. Dad's mouth is older than his brother's, but it's the same shape. You've never seen a face that matches your dad's before. You think he's about to smile, but you're not sure.

You are not sure of anything.

The pig-woman is having a party tonight, and you're all invited to come. That's why she's here, her and her blue-blond son. The boy's about your age, but he's dressed in neatly-pressed shorts and a blue, checky shirt. He is the picture of wholesome goodness. He makes you want to boak. You sense him shuffle close to mother when you come and sit in the lounge. Eyelashes pale as dust, blinking at you. Your own are caked in mascara, ringed with clotted black kohl which matches your hair gone frizzy in the sun. Your mum has hidden your crimpers (in her suitcase, under the bed; you've already used them twice, but there's been so much swimming you doubt she's even noticed).

Swimming and scowling. That's all you're good for.

Doubt the lass would rather a night out with the youngsters, eh?

The neighbour's smiling at your mum, then you. The boy recoils. You witness him visibly shrink-in small, he's folding in on himself in his need to be not there. He makes you think of a Mini Milk, melting and dipping in the middle where you've licked it. You always lick the middle, make a belt of it then chomp the solid dumbbell either end. With crisps, it is necessary to smash the bag before opening, so crumbs rain into your concave palm and Kit Kats, well, obviously you slice the tinfoil with your fingernail, snap in two silver strips, peel off the wrapper and sook each finger until you strike wafer-gold. Obviously.

Our Pete's off to a party with his girlfriend. Why don't you head out with him? Eh, Pete? Eh?

Pete is now chewing on a wasp, mutely wrestling with all the manifest reasons why this would not be a good idea, and you agree with him, you really do. You want to ring out the old with folk tied to you by blood, not the happenstance of age.

Oh, that would be lovely, wouldn't it?

Dear old mum, her tight-wide grin with that warning chime. She wants rid of your sulky coupon, wants desperately for you to enjoy yourself *like normal kids. Because it's not normal, is it?* What? Wearing Docs and a black leather jacket in the roar of an African sun? Lena's wearing a jumper over her housecoat, a great, raggedy shaggy thing, and no one bats an eyelid at her.

That's a thing you've noticed here. It is so apparent, it's scary, Stepford-wives-scary in the smooth and steady perambulation of it. It is the ability the white people have to utterly ignore. And it's not the eyes-down shuffle you get in Glasgow, when folk kid-on they can't see a jakey's begging hand. No, this is a bland blank non-acceptance of the possibility of life beyond beige-coloured skin. Delivered consistently and with precision, so you know it's not just your imagination. You've seen it in the bottle shop, with its 'In' door and its 'Out' door and its door marked 'Blacks'. Doesn't matter how many black people are queued there, they cease to exist if a white walks in. You've seen it in the silent, shameful slip from sidewalk to road as black dances white, so practised, so discrete. And you've seen your grandfather drop change into a car park attendant's hand. Your roly, jolly grandpa whose still-Kentish lilt and bawdy jokes have made you smack your lips with relish. Yes, him. The balding teddy bear you've only just met and how he dropped the coins in as if it were a bucket. That same dissociation of eye and hand and heart. Even when the attendant goes *Thank you boss*, your grandpa doesn't see him. Just drives fast and slick as lizard tongues while the man is lowering his hand.

Your gran has said the neighbours are serving haggis at the party, in honour of their Scottish guests. She's given them the recipe, though she's worried they'll not get proper pinhead here. But it will be some ersatz combination of offal and oatmeal, which is very kind. That's another weird thing. Mrs Piggy *is* very kind, has gone out of her way to make you welcome. She's so proud of her adopted homeland, almost as proud as the other-side neighbour, Mrs Van der Sandt, who has insisted you go to the Voortrekker next week. *Only if you put a chain round my neck*, you tell your mother later. You've already argued about the morality of this monument with your Uncle Pik, who has married in and would love to get another Rottweiler.

A keed like yi cannit indrstaand. Rearranging his testicles as he said it. Subtly mind, via the pockets of his shorts.

Uncle Pik will be there tonight. He's promised to bring his tuba. You look at your mum, still manically beaming, at Mrs Piggy hoicking a crumb from her teeth. Pale, pretty Pete seems enraptured with his feet, and you want, so much, to frighten him.

'Yes,' you say. 'That would be lovely.'

You go into the garden, spend the rest of the day reading, avoiding all the housework. It's daft; nobody will actually be *in* the house tonight, but there's no telling your gran. You take a sip of water, then slowly open your book. Highers soon, and you've not yet reached the close of Sunset Song. You don't want to. You are loving the journey too much, want to keep it incomplete and safe. Later, much later, you will realise this is the first time a book has moved you so completely: the language, the story, the bigger sense of it. The fact it is quite solidly and distinctively Scottish. You didn't know that writers could do that, that you were allowed to paint rhythms and cadences with your words as well as stories, and that it wasn't an affectation. It was the truth.

At the end, when it is done, you sit in your grandmother's garden. Water laps against the filter of the pool, foreign insects click and the seething liquid sun burns on, sticking the tears to your cheeks. You shudder again, again until your breathing steadies. You are crying for this girl who was the same age, had the same dreams as you and the possibility they may not happen. You are crying for the elegy of it all, and for the sudden rush of wind which rides you, smelling of cold and good damp earth. Lena sees you crying, offers an awkward smile, careful not to show her teeth. Then she goes about her business with the bins. Your gran says she has children, yet she stays here alone in the wee shed behind the bungalow, the one they call the pool house. You asked her yesterday where her children were. *Homelanma* she whispered. She gets nervous when you talk to her.

A quick shower, then it's time to PAA-AARTY! The house to yourself, they've all trouped next door already, scared in case the haggis might abscond. Well, they tend to, if you don't tether them first. If you had your own music with you, you would play it loud, but godknows what the radio's like here. The telly's bad enough. Half a channel for English speakers, and the best thing on that is Star Trek. Your mother has actually laid out a sundress on your bed. It's one she bought in Johannesburg, turquoise, ruched, with frigging elephants dancing on the hem. *Aye right*, you think, reaching for your old familiar black. This one is a dress though, a voluminous fringed affair with Afghan embroidery on the bodice. You suspect it might have come from a carpet. You steal back your crimpers, load up with hairspray and taste that crisp dry sizzle as the snakes appear. Hundreds of crinkled black snakes, jagging high and wide and spiky. The smell of burning hair and Elnett, you back-combing the crown a little to froth it up. (Straighteners have not yet been invented but, oh, when they are, what joy you'll have making those flat, poseur planes.) In case the message is not clear, you douse yourself in patchouli. Quick glance in the mirror – a teeny glance since you eschew all forms of self-appreciation. That is not the way of the individual. Wee smudge more eyeliner, winging it out like Siouxsie Sioux.

There.

You are.

A punky musky adolescent. Gothic. You raise your batwing arms. Glorious.

Milky Pete awaits downstairs. He's standing with his girlfriend, another honey-blonde. Her name is Samantha, and her dress is reddest fire. Sits like a fifties siren, curving in, flaring out. It is the skirt you want to twirl in, twirl until you're sick. She smiles with teeth that properly shine, and they are very neat, these strips of white which run, concurrently, so:

A streak of white in the mouth: *check*.

A line of white round the waist: *check*.

A flash of white on the feet: *check*.

Pete wears white socks, and this time his shirt is gridded red. He's big enough tonight for long trousers, and to extend his hand.

'Yi lk nis.'

Surprised, you shake his fingers, follow him out to his car. Samantha links her arm through yours, gushes about your hair. They ask you about Scotland. You tell them about the Mearns of Kinraddie, about the vast parks and the meagre, honest living and how rigs undulate beneath a shifting sky and the land rises up to root the standing stones. Thousands of years old, you say. Hundreds of thousands, probably.

Eet snds byitifl.

It is, you reckon. You imagine it must be. And you are furiously proud.

Gone eleven when you get to the party. It's in a massive white house, with lights in every room spilling onto the dry, rough grass where an empty pergola sits. If this was Scotland, they'd all be outside, revelling in the lack of rain, puking in the pool. Pete leads you indoors and you're suddenly shy. Lonely too; it rises like the stifling heat and slaps you in the face. Tingling cheeks, body far too hot in your truculent tent-dress. Your black clown-feet look massive beside the skittering, dainty sandals that abound. People turn to stare. This happens in Glasgow too, the sheep gawping, but they're your sheep, you've shared a lifelong diet of Irn Bru and the Sunday Post with them and when they chase you with bottles and half-hearted yells of *Haw, check oot the fuckin guisers* it doesn't feel this bad. Girls flitter past like bright, squawking birds; no-neck jocks neck their bottles, regard you with small, bleak eyes.

At first, no one approaches the huddled trio in the corner. Then some of Pete's friends come over, they bring you drinks, one asks you to dance. As he does, a familiar record jangles – it's Simple Minds. Yeah, you hate them, would die rather than dance to these sell-outs in your club up the town (they used to be called Johnny and the Self-Abusers for godsake). But they are here and so are you and you're both from bloody Glasgow! You swoop into the spangling shimmer of the music, arms wide and wild. Then Pete comes over, takes your arm. You find yourself hustled outside, Samantha scurrying after with the carry-out you brought. An older woman is shouting at you: *Inddint cim bik! We dint wint yr type hier.*

My what? you say. She repeats her angular refrain, clipping each word into your heart.

C'min. Its fien, goes Pete, opening up the car.

But what have I done wrong?

She thinks yir taeking drigs. Stupid caa. Its yir pichili, that's all. Bit she widn't listn.

Ten to twelve and you're screeching down the highway.

Wi cint hiv Higminay in a caar, huh?

You don't care. You feel withered and sick and you want your mum. There's another party they're going to try, but you ask them to drop you at gran's. One minute to midnight, you'll be fine, you say, of course you'll go next door. But you don't.

Round the back, the pool water ripples, the insomniac filter churning its own rhythm. You are worse than naked, and you can't get that feeling to return, the one where you are smug and snug in your shell. You look up at a million pinwheel stars. To be different has always been your KEEP OUT sign, it stops you getting hurt. Gives you a place to belong. Copper light glows in the sky.

Burning sky: there is a fraught haze over Alexandra. On the trellis above you, the scent of bougainvillea drips, bringing with it a distant, acrid sharpness. Across the Transvaal, you can see the gaudy shock of fireworks punching-in the witching hour. What if your difference is not your choice? What if your difference has been skinned on you since birth and it tells you: STAY OUT?

Aching, breathtakingly hot. Air clotting in your lungs, your tight sore lungs and eyes, and you're pulling at your dress. Tugging it till you are unencumbered, seizing it by the throat. You chuck it into the pool where it blooms in widow's weeds, moving without you on the surface of the water. Night licks your skin like Ewan Tavendale's kiss burned Chris. Burned you. This morning, you heard your gran tell Lena she could no longer teach her English.

You are standing in a garden, crying. In the poolhouse, the curtains shift and the world celebrates another year.

THE ART
OF ELSEWHERE

by ALI SMITH

I'VE BEEN TRYING to go elsewhere all my life.

Last year, I went all over the place. I went to Greece, I went to France, I went to Holland, I went to Morocco, I went to Canada, I went to Germany. That's just some of the places I went to. I flew, I cycled, I went on Eurostar, I went by ordinary train, I walked, I got the bus, I drove, I sat in the backs of a lot of taxis. Wherever I went, however I went, there was no getting away from it. I would put my bag down on the cobbles, or the pavement, or the grassy side of the road, or the walkway next to the canal, or the plastic-strewn beach, or the railway station plat-form, or the bed, or the folding table-thing made of canvas and aluminium that some hotels have especially for suitcases, and, where would I be?

I'd be sitting on a bench in a pretty garden high up the side of a fairly-built-up slope above the city of Naples. If you looked up you'd not see Vesuvius at all, because of the pollution. And if you looked down, you'd know Naples was down there, and you'd be able to hear the crazy hooting and roaring of the traffic, but because of the pollution it was like Naples didn't exist.

Beautiful, I'd say to myself.

I mean Rotterdam was lovely. It's got some great galleries. I particularly liked the medieval Madonna and Child with the tiny golden angels radiating out in interwoven rings round them both, playing golden musical instruments, forming a series of hoops of light, like vibrations or aura are emanating from them, and under her feet she's crushing a long thin black monstrous-looking thing, a kind of devil I suppose it's meant to be. And when I stood and looked at the painting, a painting as small as my own hand, of a pile of beautiful old books on a table and one book propped up and open at a double page, blank but for the figure of a man standing at the far end holding a spade, as if the blank pages were a field waiting to be farmed, for a moment, for a few seconds, looking at that picture, I was both right there in front of it and I was elsewhere.

Also, the gallery had a very lovely café/restaurant; there was leek soup the day I went, very nice, and even its toilets are works of art, with little plaques outside them like paintings have next to them for their title/artist information.

But pretty much the whole time I was there, I was still trying to get elsewhere.

✕

There was a girl I knew when I was at school; her name was Debbie and her dad was famously elsewhere.

That meant he was doing time, my mother told me; it was well-known among the parents that Debbie's father, from time to time, did time. Her mother worked at the petrol station where my elder brother worked the car-wash on Saturdays and Sundays, and this, along with a kindly demeanour, meant that Debbie, who was quite a tough sort of girl, and the kind who failed exams or tended to do averagely, was protective of me if I ever came under threat from the little gangs of girls who'd hang around the school gates, waiting to slap the face of a swot.

We had sewing class last thing on a Friday and for this we were seated alphabetically, which meant that Debbie and I were put next to each other. Because she knew I liked books she told me about her favourite book, which was *The Railway Children* by E Nesbit. The film is good, yeah, she said, but the book is much, much better. Then she lent me it, and was so delighted, when I gave it back to her, that I'd liked it as much as she had, that she actually did my sewing for me for weeks; she'd do her own double-quick then give me hers to hold, and work away at mine under the table, right under the sewing teacher's nose. It was the only term in my life that I ever got a good mark in sewing. Once, in an English class, our teacher, who called himself the Gaelic version of his name and was known for his ritual of firing a cannon and raising a saltire in his back garden every year at New Year, and who still wore a black gown to teach in, which no one else in the whole school did, and who always gave himself the best parts when we read Shakespeare round the class, and who despised Debbie for some reason, presumably because the staff, like the parents, knew about her dad and his doing time, told us all to open our poetry books at a poem by Rudyard Kipling called If. Then he said that the first one of us to stand up and recite, word-perfect, the whole thing off by heart could leave the class and go to lunch early.

It was the kind of cheap thing a teacher did when he didn't really want to teach the class that period. I thought about what I'd do with the time, if it was me who learned the words the fastest. Since there was nobody at home till one o'clock there'd be no point in me leaving school half an hour early, because I didn't have a key for the house and I'd have to sit in the garden until one of my parents got home from work, and the dog would hear me and start barking to get out, and anyway it was raining, but if the shed was unlocked, I could sit in the shed and wait. Okay.

But I had barely started reading the poem, barely got to the end of its second line, when someone at the back of the class pushed a chair back and stood up. We all turned.

Face the front, old Caimbeul shouted.

Facing the front, we all heard Debbie begin at the beginning. If you can keep your head when all about you. Are losing theirs and blaming it on you. I followed the poem in the book in front of me through all four of its verses. She was word-perfect. She ended at the end. You'll be a man, my son, she said.

Then she picked up her bag and walked between the desks to the front of the class.

Ah, but you didn't learn that here in this classroom today,

though, did you, em, eh, –, old Caimbeul, who was flustered and had misplaced Debbie's name, said.

My father says it into the mirror every morning when he shaves, Debbie said. And you never said anything about us not being allowed to know it already.

She swung out the door without looking back. The door clicked shut. We were all left behind.

Debbie had gone elsewhere.

Elsewhere there are no mobile phones. Elsewhere sleep is deep and the mornings are wonderful. Elsewhere art is endless, exhibitions are free and galleries are open twenty-four hours. Elsewhere alcohol is a joke that everybody finds funny. Elsewhere everybody is as welcoming as they'd be if you'd come home after a very long time away and they'd really missed you. Elsewhere nobody stops you in the street and says, Are you a Catholic or a Protestant, and when you say neither, I'm a Muslim, then says yeah but are you a Catholic Muslim or a Protestant Muslim? Elsewhere there are no religions. Elsewhere there are no borders. Elsewhere nobody is a refugee or an asylum seeker whose worth can be decided about by a government. Elsewhere nobody is something to be decided about by anybody. Elsewhere there are no preconceptions. Elsewhere all wrongs are righted. Elsewhere the supermarkets don't own us. Elsewhere we use our hands for cups and the rivers are clean and drinkable. Elsewhere the words of the politicians are nourishing to the heart. Elsewhere charlatans are known for their wisdom. Elsewhere history has been kind. Elsewhere nobody would ever say the words bring back the death penalty. Elsewhere the graves of the dead are empty and their spirits fly above the cities in instinctual, shapeshifting formations that astound the eye. Elsewhere poems cancel imprisonment. Elsewhere we do time differently.

Every time I travel, I head for it. Every time I come home, I look for it.

BECAUSE IT'S A WEDNESDAY

by A L KENNEDY

B ECAUSE IT'S A Wednesday, he's shagging Carmen.

Grotesquely unlikely name for a cleaning woman, Carmen. It doesn't even suit her as a person – entirely inappropriate, in fact. As is the shagging, of course. I am her employer – professional relationship, position of trust and so forth – I should be more restrained.

Not that a shag might not indicate trust.

I could argue that, to a degree, I am really confirming some level of interpersonal confidence.

It had started, the shagging, when Philip's office hours were cut. Inadequate warning and then he's semi-permanently home-working in the flat – emailing, drafting and whatnot – bit of a shock – while Carmen's there setting his rooms to right – polishing, ironing, folding, making his good order better and getting the place to smell of nowhere, or else like a well-maintained hotel.

Which is what I request - no trace of my having been here, no spillages, no confusions, no scent beyond fresh linen, dry heat. **Impersonal.** *People say that as if it's a bad word when it's fundamentally light and pleasant and unstressful.*

Fifth new apartment in six years – third city, third country – sustaining that level of movement, you want to feel unrestricted, stay painless, be able to slip in and out.

No pun intended.

Christ.

Old bloke shagging the help and cracking interior single entendres.

That's a bit desperate.

He stares at his hands where they're gripping her waist.

Old man's hands he has now.

How did they happen? When? Where was I?

They give the impression he's wearing ill-fitting gloves, gloves with baggy knuckles. And big, ribbed, spadey fingernails – a vulnerability about them.

And pale, pale, pale.

Carmen is wearing the pink-and-white-striped blouse today, which is his second favourite. His favourite is the green, the one she was wearing when they first shagged, when she stood up and made her move once they'd finished their cup of tea with the chocolate biscuits. This habit they'd fallen into – English habit – English being his home and this, for once, being England, or close enough – and, in consequence, there they would sit, eating these biscuits with bad, cheap chocolate on top and sharing a silent cup of tea at roughly, regularly, twelve o'clock. With no provocation, she'd leaned against the kitchen counter, given him a slightly complicated look and then raised her skirt.

Not enticing, not particularly sexual, but unmistakably a request.

She doesn't have very good English – probably thought a gesture would be more effective.

Which it was.

No idea what she actually speaks inside her head, what her language is.

Should ask to see her passport, find out.

International, me – fluent in several places, but it's English that's the big one, is dominant.

Which is a happy happenstance.

She was wearing white knickers – always does – dull from too much washing, unadorned, but somehow girlish. Surprising.

Odd when you suddenly realise that somewhere in your mind you have made an assumption about someone's underwear, even though you have at no point imagined – not even considered – that you will see it, or touch it, or pull it down and have a shag.

Shag.

She is very definitely a shag.

This isn't *fucking*, Phil's not of an age any more to *fuck*. He lacks the energy and what he thinks of as the necessary edge. And Carmen, being plain, is not *fucking* material – he has to be truthful and she truly is not.

*And we are absolutely not **making love**.*

Phil has no patience for the expression. He feels it suggests that love can be fabricated like scaffolding or a hull, or that it might be forced inside a collaborator, injected, sweated into life. He does not believe this to be the case.

Philip and Carmen *shag*.

A dogword, dogged – something comfy and tousled, sturdy, reliable, warm-muzzled, panting. You can meet its eyes and know just what you'll get. Uncomplicated.

She's bent over one of his kitchen chairs – pants and tights rumpled down to her shins, skirt lifted – lately she has let him do this, has allowed him to partly roll and partly fold it out of their way, to prevent creasing. There's a mild blush spreading on her buttocks.

Mustn't think of that, though, or I'll come too fast.

Philip is picturing railway lines and sidings, cuttings, the approach to his current city's largest railway station: overhead wires and power ducts, channels, signals, warning signs, tracks shining down to disappearing points – the naked workings of transportation, their honesty – it calms him.

He crouches against and beneath her, up her, paces himself to a steady *digdigdig*.

Dogdogdog.

Shagshagshag.

Although he needn't, he is being courteous. There absolutely is no point in holding back – she never seems to come herself, never attempts an explanation of why they do this, or what she might want. Even so, he does very often try to please her, to break a noise from her beyond the loudish rhythm of her breath. He has called her by name on a few occasions – *Carmen* – but she hasn't answered, hasn't turned her head.

Although he guesses this is not what she prefers, he tends to shag her from behind, purely because when he faces her he can't avoid being aware that she doesn't smile, avoids kissing, looks beyond his shoulder throughout as if she were puzzled by some detail, or attempting to recall an itinerant fact.

And always in the kitchen.

Domestic servant, knows her place.

Oh.

Shouldn't think of that, either. Anything hierarchical gets too horny.

He'd felt quite peculiar afterwards, on that initial afternoon – chilled and thirsty and curious, possibly affronted, but also sinking a touch into a kind of softness, a gratitude – it had been a while, after all. He'd briefly considered taking her to bed and starting again, pretending they had some meaning for each other. Carmen had only released him, dressed herself, cleared the tea things, left.

He did wonder if she'd be back, but the following Wednesday, she appeared at nine, the same as usual – only now the extra half hour added for the shag.

It had been difficult to know if he should pay her more – he was, clearly, increasing her workload, in sense, but he'd guessed any offers of extra cash would be distasteful. For a while, he'd left small gifts beside her tea mug. She ignored them. He'd begun conversations she either wouldn't, or couldn't, finish, had reached out to pat her arm when she was passing, had aimed to create an atmosphere of, if not tenderness, then positive regard, but she seemed to dislike this and as a result he had taken to rushing a roll of notes at her when the month ended and being vague about how much he genuinely owed, overestimating as if by accident.

I can afford it. Afford her.

Oh.

Not yet, though.

Oh.

One day she'll make me think of additional vowels.

Meanwhile, divert myself.

Affording.

Comforts.

Luxuries.

Pleasant situations.

Yes. Right up to the walls I am most pleasantly situated and living well within my means, living well completely.

When he'd viewed it, the flat was already exhaustively furnished and equipped – carpets, bed sheets, towels, ornaments, pictures, cutlery, pans, reading glasses, candles, lampshades, soap – as if the owners had left on holiday and had asked him to stay and take care of their belongings. Generously vacant for him – sign the inventory and he was home.

Mine.

My floor, my wall, my window, my view.

Outside it's easing into spring. Blossom shivers in the tall, haphazard trees and young light is being kind to the buildings opposite, the thin lane that runs beside them.

Foxes in that lane at night. I can hear them. Foxes in the city, and rabbits and hawks – the countryside's cleaned, it's shriven – but here there's hunting day and night. There are screams – exactly like women. In the morning I see traces.

He can feel heat running at the backs of his legs, the strain of the end on its way and he studies the shop fronts, clings to them for a beat and a beat and beat.

Flower shop – no one goes in it, not properly an area for flowers, not yet. Refurbished café – one of those chains. 24 hour grocers and off-licence. Tobacconist's. Chemist. Somewhere that's still empty – whitewashed windows, dust.

He can see from the broad, slanted outlines left on the sandstone that the business was called Zumzum – silly name – typical.

No way of knowing what they sold, probably fancy cloth, or gold jewellery, maybe weird, small, cubic sweets, the kinds of stuff those people liked. Butcher – sausages, pork pies, nice bit of steak for the weekend – have to support your local butcher. Funny lettering over the door from when it was different, stocked different meat. Cheap paint, it'll fade.

Transitional areas. Reclamations. They start off unsteady, blanks where you wouldn't expect them, oddities, reminders, and then in the end, everything fades. You get a new community. Peace.

And, before the disruptions settle and the fresh life grows, you can roll in and get a cheap flat with all the trimmings.

My street, this is – in my neighbourhood – my house in my street in my neighbourhood.

And my view, my window, my wall, my floor, my chair, my shag.

My shag.

Oh.

My shag.

Oh.

Possession.

Oh.

Does the trick.

Oh.

Quite.

Phil draws himself away from her, removes the condom.

Can't be too careful.

He's pressed her forward and her blouse has ridden up. For a moment he has to stare at the scarring on her back – purplish-red and swollen. Then she straightens, hides it. He's never been able to see the whole of it.

Burning.

Beating.

Some wrongness.

Some wrong act.

He bins his little parcel of semen, the tepid crush of what he's left, and adjusts himself, clears his throat. He's sticky, needs a shower and maybe an aspirin, but he can't enjoy either until Carmen's gone, in case he gives offence. This means he can only loiter and wait for his pulse to dim, keep his hands from rising to his face, because they will smell of activities and people, needs, heats.

By the far table leg, he notices there are crumbs – he must have dropped a sizeable piece of biscuit and then trampled it into a mess while he was busied.

Dirty old man.

He inspects the bottom of his shoe – more biscuit.

Tsk.

That being the noise of crushed biscuit.

When she turns, respectable again, he points to the mess and notices what could be a mild warmth in her expression, a certain friendliness towards the idea of sweeping. Before she goes for the pan and brush, she upends both the shagging chair and Philip's ordinary chair and rests them on the table.

He's seen it before, of course – Carmen, too. Someone with a clear, dark hand has inked a surname and a date on the underside of each seat. There is a liquid, foreign taste about the script, not unattractive. Philip knows – having, late one night, eventually checked his furniture – that the same date and name has been written on the back of his dresser, the head board of his bed, under his sofa, somewhere on every chair, beneath lamp stands, inside cupboards where the doorframes make a shadow. He is almost, almost, almost surrounded by a multiplicity of records, marks.

In the spring of last year.

Before they left.

Some morning, probably morning – early hours most suitable for clearing out.

Blossoms through the window and closed shops.

Making a good order better for everyone.

Goodbye. Goodbye. Goodbye.

Didn't even take their nail clippers, or the thermos flask.

How strange it must have been to be so unimpeded. Like falling.

Carmen tidies round him, then quietly empties the tea leaves out of the pot and – as it happens – probably onto the condom.

She rights the chairs and he sits, a little light-headed. She washes the crockery which was here when he arrived and dries it with the tea towel which was rolled neatly with some others in a drawer – scenes of village life, British sea birds, common knots, blue and white checks, red and white checks, plain blue.

Once she's done, Carmen walks to stand close at his side, eases her scrubbed and tidy fingers inside his jacket, finds his pocket and takes out his comb, his own personal comb.

He exhales, with the intention that she will feel it.

And then he lets her.

He lets her comb his hair – run the little teeth back from his forehead, over his temples, smooth him from his hairline to his nape, and he drops his face forward and nods, indicating that she should continue, and sometimes they do this for twenty minutes, for half an hour, or until he forgets, until he fades, until he's simple.

It helps.

It definitely helps.

SULLIVAN'S ASHES

by ALAN WARNER

MYSELF, COUSIN JOHN, Sullivan's third wife Aileen and the sergeant all sat together in the police station at Tobermory. We read once more the photocopied clause in Sullivan's will:

I wish for no funeral service but to be cremated privately and then for my ashes to be spread from the specific silver urn, by a semi-naked and beautiful woman, galloping a white horse across the sands of Calgary Bay, Isle of Mull – irrespective of expense, inclement weather and the challenge of finding a beautiful woman on Mull.

'Aye. He had to get that last wee dig in, right to the bitter end,' said Aileen – the only native among us.

We looked to the sergeant, a pleasant and practical man. But new to the job.

'It's not an urn. It's his bashed up old champagne bucket from The Grand in Brighton,' Cousin John revealed.

'Yes,' said Aileen. 'And if it hadn't been full quite so often, he might have had something to leave me. Us.'

'But it said here he's leaving you the bucket.' John rustled the pages to quote it.

Aileen gave Cousin John a hard look. 'I'll use it too, once I'm rid of his leftovers.'

Practical as ever, the sergeant asked, 'How are you to keep the ashes in a champagne bucket, with the great probability of a howling gale?'

Quickly, Cousin John said, 'I was thinking a good dose of yon kitchen clingfilm stuff over the top, and the lassie can pierce it with her long fingernails?'

The sergeant and I both nodded, though we all felt Cousin John was getting a bit ahead of the game. He went on, 'And we'll need Doc Fraser standing by. To treat the lassie for frostbite. Best if we get a healthy young lassie. One of them strip-o-grams. They stand up best to the cold. I respect those lassies.'

Aileen said, 'I don't want the doctor there and I doubt he'll attend. Sullivan never invited him back up to the poker evening, not when he got the house off him but after he stopped prescribing those sleeping pills.'

'So you intend to proceed?'

'This is what we wanted to ask, Sergeant. From a legal point of view. The possible ramifications?'

'Round here, that could depend on exactly how...' he flicked the page and read aloud, ' 'semi-naked' any young lady actually is.'

'Topless,' Cousin John demanded.

I said, 'On Mull, semi-naked is a bikini.'

'A bikini doesn't break any law. Topless might be indecent exposure. It's certainly exposure, in this climate.'

Aileen took another Dunhill out her pack and told us, a bit nostalgically, 'On Mull, semi-naked is a skirt above the knee. Can I smoke in here?'

'I'm afraid not,' said the policeman.

'Couldn't you lock me in one of your cells, Sarge? I'd even close the peephole.'

I gave Aileen a look. She wasn't a day under fifty-five but still well-preserved and hopelessly flirty. The sergeant ignored her. What can you say about Aileen? Her life was like all those Dolly Parton songs. Or maybe just one: *Down From Dover*.

I said, 'So we have a week or so.'

Cousin John pondered, 'Unless we wait to watch the weather. For the sake of the beautiful lassie on the horse?'

Aileen erupted. 'I'm no having Sullivan's ashes waiting up in that house. They'd crawl out and make for the drinks cabinet. Why the hell couldn't he have them scattered off the South Downs in a gentle English breeze?'

The sergeant looked troubled now. He stood. 'I might need to phone Edinburgh about all this.' Then he thought aloud to himself. 'But what department?'

'Another thing.' The cousin held up a pointed finger – and he was a farmer. 'There's no a white horse on this whole island.'

'Oh good god,' Aileen groaned. 'Use a Highland cow.'

'It'll no gallop,' the cousin shot back, in a voice revealing too much experience in such a matter.

✕

Aileen, Cousin John and I drove back up the tiered roads to Sullivan's modern holiday bungalow, high above the bay. In the disused connecting garage sat the scandalous American pool table.

The house had been won off Sullivan by Doc Fraser in a two day poker marathon years before, to legally pass to the doctor at the time of Sullivan's death. The doc had already been up to measure for new carpets.

Plumpton, the fat cat – named after the Sussex racecourse – sat by a bowl on the kitchen floor. He'd brought round some semi-feral acquaintances for a meal. Four of the beggars. They all sat, turning their snooty heads expectantly. Aileen stamped her heel and there was a rough scuffle around the catflap as all five fought to exit first. 'Wait till the good doctor deals with you,' she screamed.

Cousin John said, 'Fred Pinder over on the mainland has a stables. Supplies horses to them movies that come venturing up round here. He can get you a whole bloody cavalry troop. He'll bring you over a unicorn in his horse box.'

✕

Sullivan never passed a penny on a pavement without picking it up. He had been Sussex-born and bred. He owned this long playing record, *Old Songs of Sussex: Agricultural Labourers' Ballads*

From Both Sides of the Downs. I loved that: 'Both Sides.' I wanted to ask the doc if I could inherit the disc.

In the seventies and eighties, Sullivan had made his money from slot machines in Brighton and Eastbourne. One time I asked him what it was like as a livelihood. *'Brighton Rock* meets parking meters,' was all I got.

Aileen once told me that Sullivan collected the coins in straining plastic buckets every night of the week and loaded them into his Volvo hatchback. The rear suspension broke. Apparently there were one hundred and fifty unused mops in Sullivan's Brighton garage.

A *What the Butler Saw* machine still stood in the front lounge at ten pence a go. I'd have loved to have inherited that too, but the doc had got the house contents as well in a later poker game.

Sullivan had fallen in love with Mull after just one drive around it. He must have seen Calgary Bay for the first time that very day. I never once heard of him going round the island again, so it made an impression.

Above Tobermory, Sullivan's fine view over the bay and across the Sound of Mull, our poker evenings and those few winning dinners at the Western Isles Hotel seemed enough.

I once asked Sullivan why he loved it up on the island so much and he swung open all the bay windows. 'Listen,' he yelled. 'Just silence, isn't it? It's the elsewhere. When you're an Englishman you have England and you have... elsewhere. And you have to pay to get elsewhere, sonny boy.'

✗

That first winter of westerly gales, silence was in short supply. The poker games were interrupted affairs. The tiles rattled on Sullivan's roof like a miked-up marimba. We watched the molehills actually slide across his lawn and up the slope where they tipped into his fish pond. The herons had taken all the goldfish. On the third day of gales, a baffled young thrush came down the chimney and immediately broke its neck on the inside window pane. Sullivan took it to the kitchen and de-suctioned the backdoor open: that dead bird flew one last time, off the end of the shovel and heading east, at sixty miles an hour.

Plumpton's lock-less catflap had been going mental, like the chattering teeth of some giant. It had to be sealed with electrical tape which puffed and salivated. Sullivan didn't venture up for many winters after that.

When I returned to the isle one week after our meeting at the police station, I was not alone in the bar of the car ferry.

Fred Pinder had often phoned from his stables and sensibly suggested stunt women from the film industry. Portraits had been e-mailed to Cousin John. But none of these women passed his strict criteria.

There I was on that early boat with Fred Pinder in his vintage SNP t-shirt. And with Miss Zoë Murphy, a third year Dramatic Arts student from Coatbridge. Coatbridge Sunnyside, she emphasised.

Zoë had told me she wanted to be in musicals but this assignment seemed like a strange first step. We paid her seven hundred

cash upfront, but she still insisted she'd throw in some pole dancing, of which she'd done plenty to supplement her student grant.

Every person in the ferry's bar stared at Zoë in her fluffy blue,
fake fur jacket – even the women. I believed someone was going
to approach her for an autograph.

When the vessel came into the Firth of Lorn, spray smashed
the bar windows like shampoo suds on a shower cubicle and the
boat dipped from bow to stern. After ten minutes Zoë headed for
the toilets.

Fred Pinder was drinking whisky with Irn Bru and he leaned
across. 'I'm away down to see if they'll let me check Blade isn't
kicking the back of his box out.'

'I don't think she can ride. Can we sit her on the horse in the
box first, for a wee try out?'

Fred said, 'No. You pay me for the horse. I'm nothing to do
with any rider.'

After Fred had gone, bare-footed Zoë swayed back to my
table. She'd taken off her heels and carried them by the straps in
one hand. The make-up and the tanning salon were all in vain up
against the tossing Firth. Her beautiful young face was grey as
steak.

'Look. I know you swore you could, but you're not like all
those other actresses, are you? Water-ski, snowboard, speak Pol-
ish, ride a motorcycle and horse?'

'Ah can ski. I've been to Chamonix.'

'Horses though. Sure you can... canter a horse, hands-free in a
force ten? Even a wee trot maybe?'

'I've a nice bikini. Did plenty gymkhana when I was wee;

rosettes all over my bedroom wall in Coatbridge. Sunnyside. We're no gonna sink are we? Has this boat sunk before?' She looked fearfully around the panorama. 'Look at all they mountain things. We've mountains in North Lanarkshire too. I climbed one when I was a wee lassie.'

'Really? What one?'

'One of they slag heaps from the old coal mines.'

She soon returned to the toilet with her arms held out horizontally. She'd left her high heels upright on the table and they fell to their sides and spilled my coffee.

Word travels fast on the dark island. At the ferry terminal, five boy racer cars were drawn up broodily in their usual row. Observing exactly who disembarked. I noted the car windows were all open; the young male drivers and passengers shouted excitedly through those aligned windows, like some antiquated telegraph system.

Those five cars followed my hire car and Fred, towing his horse box, up the road all the way to Tob'.

Zoë had sunglasses on next to me. 'I feel all famousy already,' she told me. 'I'll just put on a wee touch more cheesy lipstick.' She wound down her window and her shades blew off.

Around Sullivan's ashes – in the champagne bucket sealed by clingfilm – there was a party going on up at the bungalow. All our old poker crew was there. Aileen was drunk and repeatedly played *No Tears (In The End)* by Roberta Flack on the hi-fi. Disturbingly though, Aileen was only dancing with Doc Fraser.

Zoë furrowed her brow at the turning vinyl and actually asked me, 'This isnie a CD. How's this thing make music?'

Cameron, that wannabe journalist, was there and he kept trying to interview Zoë, telling her it was for the Island Arts Newsletter. Then Cousin John arrived, already in black tie. He studied Zoë from a distance in a shy but still unhealthy manner then crossed over to me and whispered, 'Aye. Good long fingernails there for the clingfilm.'

Zoë sneaked back to the bathroom yet again. Then she appeared next to Doc Fraser and crying Aileen.

Zoë tapped the doc on his shoulder. Johnny Cash was singing *Melva's Wine* which never failed to make Aileen weep. Zoë showed the doc something and suddenly the couple broke off from dancing and the threesome headed back to the bathroom and locked the door. I became fearful that drug use had reared its ugly head – imported into our poker circle by Zoë – or perhaps practices which were even more unspeakable.

But soon the doc emerged and drew me aside from the melee. 'That daft wee lassie you've got can't ride any horses tomorrow.'

'Why not?'

'She's months pregnant.' He held up one of those white plastic testers with two blue lines. 'She's been spewing up then peeing on these all day with the same result. I didn't even examine her. And I *could* have,' he winked.

'For god's sake.'

Fred Pinder was listening and he laughed, but Cousin John didn't take it well at all. Then there was a fearful crying scene. Aileen comforted Zoë and phone calls were made to a startled suitor in Coatbridge. Sunnyside.

Some of those boy racer cars presumptuously drew up outside. The young men with shaved heads were unable to choose between the pool table or hovering round Zoë, but when they found the doc had already confiscated all the pool balls they immediately gravitated to Zoë. When they learned of her condition they swiftly re-gravitated and fed coins into the *What the Butler Saw* machine.

'Ach well, Sullivan would be happy business is still ticking over,' Cousin John said and he nodded at the silver champagne bucket.

Another hour and Zoë was slow-dancing mournfully with one of the young bloods. And very soon they cajoled her off down the hill to the bars. What did I care? All was lost.

Meanwhile, Aileen had retired to her marital chambers with Doc Fraser, even before we threw the last of the poker crew out.

Cousin John whispered in my ear, 'Well well. Looks like Aileen's continued residence is assured.'

I nodded, noticing one of Zoë's white testers, upright in an empty glass like a cocktail stick.

From my sleeping bag, at half four in the morning, I heard Zoë come back alone and go into the spare room. Yet through the wall, she mumbled several times, tantalisingly. I feared she was with Cousin John and, half in jealousy, I arose to find John – not for the first time – asleep on the pool table in his shirt and tie, escaping the draughts.

Zoë was sharing her bed with Plumpton the cat. 'I suppose you want your money back?' She stroked the old purr box.

'No, dear. You get yourself a good fast pram.'

The next morning, the scandal firing around the island even reached my ears. Zoë had been unable to find a pole but had danced around an erect brush handle in the Mishnish then collected donations for her cause.

Calgary Bay is a noble location to spread your ashes. I can recommend it. Facing the infinite west, a cup of sparkling sand with jaws of rock protecting it – normally the sea glows chlorinated blue in at the rock edges, magnifying arm-thick ropes of kelp ten feet under the surface. It looks like a better place down there. That shade of blue would normally have matched the aquamarine lines on Zoë's pregnancy tester. However, on that morning, turbulent swell was bursting forward from the sea in long and creamy rolls.

Up on the road a considerable audience had gathered, sheltering shamefully behind the windscreens of their cars, mobile phones and high definition camcorders ready.

With a long telephoto lens, old Shutters Stuart from *The Port*

Star was lurking about for a photo to accompany his inevitable article. If Zoë had reached the saddle he'd probably have tried to sell it on to *The Scottish Sun*. But now he was in for a grim disappointment.

Our poker crew sheltered behind the horse box, around Mister Blade, Pinder's beautiful white mare. The horse was saddled up, her ears flattened against the wind. Fred held her by the bridle and I was glad young Zoë couldn't climb on; it was such a powerful-looking creature.

The sergeant, Cousin John, Zoë (with a hot water bottle under her fake fur jacket), and Doc Fraser – his arm round Aileen – all fearfully studied the impatient beast.

'Nothing for it,' Aileen stated. 'I've got my Wonderbra on, though I haven't rid a horse in twenty year.'

Cousin John curled his nose. 'That's breach of contract.'

'Don't you listen to him, beautiful,' Doc Fraser told her. 'You'll be as grand as Charlton Heston, riding up the sands in *El Cid* and if you take a wee tumble? Well, I'm a doctor.'

I shook my head, squinted out to sea, then walked down to the water's edge. The sergeant then Cousin John joined me.

'Aileen's going to break her neck,' the policeman assured us. 'I really can't allow it.'

'Aye. It's terrible. A Wonderbra. It's breach of contract. She's attractive but she's not beautiful. Sullivan wouldn't approve. And her smelling of the doc's Old Spice too.'

'Help us out Sergeant.' I pointed far into the water, towards the mighty west.

They ignored us for a good spell then intuited a uniform and so reluctantly they came in, brought to our waving arms by the rollers. Two young men and two young women, rising out from the salt water, surfboards stuffed under their arms.

'What's the problem? There's no restrictions here,' shouted one man, wiping his mouth. He was offended as all our eyes turned directly to the young lady standing beside him in her wet suit.

Cousin John opened his mouth, 'It's Venus on the half-shell. Ask and ye *shall* receive.'

'In the name of the law of this island, what are you wearing under that?' the sergeant pointed.

'I beg your ruddy pardon? I thought this was the twenty-first century.'

'What are you wearing under that?'

The girl looked at her friends then back at the sergeant. 'That it's your business, just a bikini.'

Cousin John yelled, 'Ever ridden a horse?'

She was Australian, twenty-two and tanned all over, hair bleached by open skies. She had ridden bareback horses since childhood and fifty quid clinched it.

She and Blade started at the far end of the beach and came back down along that surf line toward us, hooves smashing up puffs of spray as she leaned back in the stirrups.

Up and down the sand, out the flashing silver champagne bucket and freed from the young woman's clutch, old Sullivan spread himself across our beautiful beach, each scatter like struggling, final heartbeats as he passed off quite gloriously into some new kind of elsewhere.

The Elsewhere collection was commissioned by the Edinburgh International Book Festival, thanks to a generous grant from Creative Scotland and the Scottish Government's Edinburgh Festivals Expo Fund. In an innovative publishing and design partnership, Glasgow-based publisher Cargo and San Francisco-based publisher McSweeney's have produced the Elsewhere box set of four themed volumes.

EDINBURGH INTERNATIONAL BOOK FESTIVAL
Commissioning editors: Nick Barley, Sara Grady, Roland Gulliver
Copy editors: Jennifer Richards, Oisín Murphy-Lawless
Thanks to: Amanda Barry, Andrew Coulton, Elizabeth Dunlop,
Helen Moffat, Nicola Robson, Kate Seiler, Janet Smyth

edbookfest.co.uk

CARGO
Publishing director: Mark Buckland
Managing editor: Helen Sedgwick
Thanks to: Alistair Braidwood, Martin Brown, Rodge Glass,
Brian Hamill, Craig Lamont, Anneliese Mackintosh, Gill Tasker

cargopublishing.com

McSWEENEY'S
Design and art direction: Brian McMullen,
Adam Krefman, Walter Green
Illustrations: Jack Teagle
Thanks to: all at McSweeney's

mcsweeneys.net

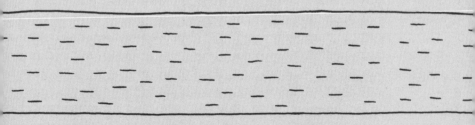